LOOKING
IN

Nicole,

EnJOY the
journey!

Tii

Discover, Define and Align the True Value
of Your Life, Leadership and Legacy

LOOKING
IN

TRACI PHILIPS

For permission requests, write to the author at
traci@theinnatecoach.com. For additional contact
with the author, contact the publisher at
jennifer@brightcommunications.net.
Internet addresses were accurate at the time the book went to
press.
Printed in the United States of America
Published in Hellertown, PA
Cover and interior design and illustrations by Leanne Coppola
Library of Congress Control Number: 2021911796
ISBN 978-1-952481-33-8
2 4 6 8 10 9 7 5 3 1 paperback

Bright
COMMUNICATIONS

Contents

Foreword

IN THE BEGINNING, THERE WAS ONLY YOU: YOUR MOST AUTHENTIC, BRILLIANT AND SHINING SELF. The perfect and unconditional you, unblemished by fears and doubts. At the opening of your story and not yet tainted by the stories gifted to you by people around you, by experiences, by culture and by the world. You were nothing but what Traci Philips calls your "Zone of Brilliance."

You were wide awake and ready to fully awaken to life and the world, and then it happened ... the conditioning. As Traci describes it, "From the moment we are born, the conditioning begins." The process of moving away from unconditional love and self-acceptance to conditional love and self-doubt.

This condition typically happens without us even knowing, and while it only rarely leaves external marks, it leaves deep cuts and grooves on the inside. And as we continue our life journey, we begin to sense the conditioning and we certainly feel the painful impacts of this conditioning.

As we often do when we're in pain, we seek to diminish, mask or cover up the pain. We medicate ourselves and our lives with anything to distract us from the questions: "Is this all there is?" "Is this all I am?" And these questions alone often cause us to feel even more pain and uncertainty, so we protect ourselves by going into what Traci calls the "deep sleep."

What we often call a midlife crisis is actually a midlife awakening, when the voice of our authentic brilliance cries out to be released and unleashed into the world. But there's so much pressure to be a certain way, to perform a certain way, to live a life of having over being. Traci Philips' *Looking In* is your answer to the cries of your authentic brilliance.

Boldly leaning into her own personal journey of awakening and awareness, Traci shares the pain and triumph of her own experience. Most important, she invites each of us to take our own journey inside. To turn our back on our role choices and to vulnerably embrace our soul choices. To dump our comparing and judging against others and to lift up our own brilliance and value.

In what must be the awakening of the times, Traci shines a light on the voice of our imposter syndromes. That voice that whispers words of doubt and unworthiness into our heads, which clashes with the truth and wisdom of your soul's voice that shouts "You ARE enough!" Here lies the great choice — choose to try to drown out or silence the voice with all forms of distraction and medication OR choose to follow this voice inside to learn and grow past it. *Looking In* is your essential map for this journey.

Author and spiritualist Joseph Campbell is widely credited with this insight and warning: "The cave you fear to enter holds the treasure you seek." In *Looking In*, Traci Philips gives us tools to use for our inward journey as she reminds us of all that is innate and authentic. In short, the possibility of us.

Looking In reminds us of the longing we all share to create a legacy based upon the impact and imprint we leave in and on everything and everyone we interact with. Traci reminds us that impact is not optional, but the nature of impact is the outcome of our choices, our courage, our willingness to leap, and the inside work we're willing to do.

In reading *Looking In* and its empowering message, I was reminded of Viktor Frankl's profound book *Man's Search for Meaning* where he encourages us that no matter what our circumstances (in his case, losing nearly his entire family and surviving the concentration camps): "Forces beyond your control can take away everything you possess except one thing, your freedom to choose how you will respond to the situation. You cannot control what happens to you in life, but you can always control what you will feel and do about what happens to you."

Let's face it: We all crave control, but we've been conditioned to pursue control by trying to control our environment and avoiding our work. And then came the COVID pandemic which harshly and abruptly shattered our false sense of control. Traci reminds us that we control so very little—nothing outside of ourselves. Yet we can have the ultimate control when we choose to embrace our own choices.

Not willing to simply offer us tools and perspectives, Traci challenges each of us to embrace this mantra for our lives … Own You! All of you … the brilliant and beautiful, the dark and shadowy, the confident and the uncertain, perfectly imperfect spiritual beings living a human experience.

Traci invites you to unleash all of YOU into the world. She challenges us to ask not if we're able, but are we willing … to trust ourselves, to take the risk, to journey into the cave of our souls … wading into the deep end of our lives, our brilliance, and our possibilities for impact in the world.

This is what Traci offers each of us in *Looking In*. Stop waiting for the world to change because when you change your perspectives, the world changes in front of your eyes. As it has been said, seeing is not believing … believing is seeing.

Looking In is Traci Philips' loving invitation to believe in yourself even when you aren't certain. To love yourself even when you don't feel loveable. To trust yourself even if you doubt your trustworthiness. To empower yourself even when you don't feel powerful.

Most important, Traci blesses you with the truth that you are enough, that you are trustworthy, that you are brilliant, that you are worthy, that you are the hero you've been waiting for your whole life.

See you on the inside!

—Jeff Nischwitz
Inspirational Speaker, Transformation Coach and Snow Globe Shaker
Author of *Unmask*, *Arrows of Truth* and *Just One Step*

Author's Note

THIS BOOK IS DEDICATED TO ALL OF THE PEOPLE WHO HAVE POURED INTO ME OVER THE YEARS AND WHO HAVE CHEERED ME ON AND SUPPORTED ME.

A special dedication goes to my daughter, Madison, who has always been my shepherd to personal growth and exceptional leadership, by expecting the best I can give, graciously pointing out where I fall short and loving me, regardless.

We're all playing roles in each other's plays. Sometimes, we are called to be a supporting role, other times, a villain. Yet, whatever role we play, large or small, temporary or long-term, we do so in order for the person whose play we are in to have the life lessons and experiences they seek. We dedicate blood, sweat and tears to our roles. We play them to the very best of our abilities, striving for the final curtain call and that standing ovation. It is at this point where our souls know we came together to support a life worthy of being called a Legacy.

For this reason, you will see this book is divided into Acts.

Enjoy the show!

SETTING THE STAGE
Waking Up

"A crucial challenge is to stop treating disillusionment as a problem or something negative, and use it as an awakening force. To be disillusioned is to see through the illusion, in conjunction with releasing its hold on us. We, thus, become disenchanted, no longer spellbound by our conditioning. We are far more able to skillfully approach our edge. As such, disillusionment is a kind of sobriety, a catalyst for waking up, a great opportunity."

—Robert Masters

WAKING UP CAN BE CHALLENGING. Depending on how deeply we have been asleep and how attached we are to our slumber, awakening can cause a sense of disorientation, confusion, grumpiness and even anger.

Of course, it does depend on HOW we are awakened. Is it a gentle touch and the words, "Time to wake up," softly spoken in our ear? Or is it a harsh, blaring alarm jolting us into consciousness?

However we are awakened, the fact we are being asked to wake up is because it is time. Something within is nudging us and telling us the hour is now to come to our senses and awareness, to be actively and meaningfully engaged in what is going on around us.

This call to awaken is asking for us to begin the process of becoming more intentionally purposeful and responsible to what we came to our lives to do, be and build.

How long might we have played the defensive game where our focus has been on reacting to what comes at us, and our mission has been to protect ourselves and what's important to us by blocking and tackling what threatens us?

What if, instead, we are being awakened to the opportunity to engage offensively, where we call the plays and direct where we want the ball to go? What if we are to decide and determine how we want to experience the game and create our legacy?

What if we are waking up to learn the process of becoming Sovereign and Authentically Aligned? What if we are being invited to a place where we can finally see and act clearly because we are coming from a true sense of congruency within ourselves? What if awakening is ultimately about owning who we are, how we think and what we are here to contribute, not from a place of external expectation, but from a space of internal knowing?

If this is the case, then we would need to, first, come out of the deep sleep we have been in that has kept us from this ownership process.

Without a doubt, we have all lived in a world that has conditioned us to consider things based on that which is outside of ourselves. This indoctrination has influenced us to adopt lifestyles that are fixated on results and driven by the rules of categorization and the measured value of others. In truth, our lives are to be appreciated based on what we have within us, what we have, personally, experienced and developed in the world, and what we have yet to create.

In Paulo Coelho's book *The Alchemist,* he states, "There is only one way to learn. It's through action. Everything you need to know you have learned through your journey. Remember that wherever your heart is, there you will find your treasure. You've got to find the treasure, so that everything you have learned along the way can make sense."

The treasure Coelho speaks of is our innate value, what is within us that is unique and held only by us. That treasure IS our gift to the world.

Waking up allows for a better understanding of what our treasure is and how to define this for ourselves and own it, more fully, in our lives. Navigating this path of discovery leads us to better understand, as Coelho mentions, what value our heart plays in this process. Yet, it is not our heart, alone, that offers the information we seek.

In her book *Three Brains,* Karen Jensen discusses the connection between our head, heart and gut. Most cultures have trained us away from the heart "brain" (how we feel) and the gut "brain" (what we sense) and into the head "brain" (what we think), alone. The head is where ego resides and where the information that comes from outside of us is held. We have been acculturated to live from the head, measuring our value based on intellectual intelligence, money, status, power, proof, security and others' opinions. Building entire civilizations that live from this place has cost us much.

So, we are awakening.

The soft, gentle nudges of our own inner awareness — the truth of our innate value and the information that our heart and gut have to share — may have gone unheard and unacknowledged for a very long time. Maybe we have had moments of "wake up," but we have decided to turn over and go back to sleep — choosing the conditioning of what is comfortable, known and "safe." Maybe we have opted to tune out the inner noise altogether, and we have never stirred at all.

So, the alarm volume has been turned up, over the years, and has become louder and louder.

Now, we may find ourselves experiencing the shrill and jarring sounds of the Wake-Up Call. What our hearts and guts have to share must be heard! The real reason we came here must be realized.

Perhaps you are waking up and viewing your current conditions as harsh and sudden. Much of what you have trusted to be your places of certainty and security are no longer felt to be safe and stable. Maybe, you are finally seeing they actually never truly were.

Seemingly, everywhere you turn, things are falling apart and coming undone. There is discomfort. Unfathomable truths may be coming to light. There is inner unrest and fear.

As leaders, first of ourselves, and then of others, we no longer have the luxury of hitting the snooze button. If there is transformational change happening, it's game time! The players have already begun to enter the field. We no longer have a choice of if we are going to be one of them or if we will be on the bench or in the stands, watching. If we are feeling upheaval in our lives, our number is being called. Our only choice is HOW we will enter and play the game.

In his book *Unmask: Let Go of Who You're Supposed to Be & Unleash Your True Leader*, Jeff Nischwitz discusses how true leaders reframe the old-school concept of courage, "Far from avoiding or ignoring them, conscious leaders acknowledge their fears and questions, yet confidently and decisively take action and lead others through the difficult or challenging times, thereby demonstrating courage through their authenticity."

Nischwitz speaks of courage. This word derives from the Latin word *cor,* meaning heart. Here, again, we see it takes the wisdom of our emotional center to lead and live fully.

Considering this and the fact that how we choose to act in our lives is significantly affected by how we feel, how we react to our awakening, each of us, will not only have an impact on us, but will greatly impact others.

Depending on our level of personal influence, how we handle ourselves through reconstruction and renovation can create lasting internal and external change and consequences.

As I see it, we are in this together. We truly always have been. We were created as mirrors for one another to challenge and support the growth we each seek individually, and the evolution that we seek collectively. I love considering the Martin Luther King Jr. quote, "We must learn to live together as brothers or perish together as fools."

In any time of uncertainty, revolution and transition, we want to be aware that we are not in this alone. Therefore our reverence towards others matters. As things shift, some may still be choosing their course of action. We each move in our own time, and we can only individually decide where we are in all of it for ourselves. It takes great awareness, patience and courage not to want of others what we want for ourselves. We may want others to act as we act; otherwise, we tell ourselves the story they are acting wrongly or not acting at all.

Sometimes, support looks different. Sometimes, it is building, and we don't even know it. Some people are comfortable reacting quickly, while others choose to step back, reflect and eventually act from places that may not be evident, the way everyone else is doing it or the way you are doing it.

During times of adjustment, we get to be careful to not form the very judgment we would not want from others.

Some of the best research of our time around the causes and impact of shame was conducted by social researcher, speaker and author Brené Brown. Her extensive findings have shown us that shame is a powerful thing. It can shut people down and have them acting in very inhuman ways. It can cause them to be aggressive and controlling. It can also keep people frozen and unsure of how to act.

When we are too quick to judge others based on our interpretation of their actions, we risk escalating the culture of blame and shame. This limits us from moving and leading forward into truth and solution. This is especially important for us to acknowledge during times of increased instability and uncertainty, which tend to trigger shame. Therefore adding more of it will only perpetuate and deepen the current experience.

We also want to be intentional not to try to save or too quickly fix the discomfort we are feeling, lest we repeat the approach and actions of the past that have created the place in which we now find ourselves that is needing to change.

It takes time sitting in the discomfort and unknowing to allow ourselves the room to open up to the new and undiscovered parts within us. Only here will we find the answers that are right and true for us.

I believe that in any environment where things are shifting, we can at least recognize that all is not what it seems. Beneath the surface and what may look obvious, there is always something wonderful and exciting waiting to emerge, enlighten and innovate.

How can you look at this time in your life as one of healing, self-discovery and breakthrough? Can you fathom that what you are experiencing as difficult and challenging is actually a glorious opportunity to do things differently and be more authentic and powerful? What if massive change is what is needed for ultimate growth and advancement to occur? Think and feel into where you are right now. What is possible that wasn't before?

Can you commit to leaning into what you are experiencing and courageously allow for the unknown to meet you where you are? What can you do to take small steps in this direction?

I appreciate what Gay Hendricks shares in his book *The Big Leap* around commitment and Zone of Genius (the innate place of brilliance within you). "Commitment works as a springboard to your Zone of Genius. The moment you make a sincere commitment to living in your Zone of Genius, you propel yourself in that direction. Once you're in the zone, commitment also works magnificently well as a steering mechanism and calibration device to keep you centered there."

Of course, this starts with truly seeing, hearing and understanding who we are. Ask yourself this: What IS my Zone of Genius? If I don't know who I am and what I was made to offer, how can I possibly see, hear and understand others for who they truly are? How can I effectively lead from my rightful position and make a positive, lasting impact?

For this, we get to speak, listen and process. We get to acknowledge, through each of our stories of experience, what we haven't, thus far. We get to do this from a place of openness, caring and patience. In times of change, there is a lot to sort through and understand. We get to give ourselves the time it takes.

We (and others in our world) may be waking up. It may take a bit of time before we can legitimately act due to confusion, surprise and overwhelm.

What I feel is this: When we are met with extreme change and restructuring in our lives, it's for a reason. The situation is not meant to simply go away. It is there to build us by creating a force that will make room for what is meant to be seen.

The last thing we would want to do is go back to sleep.

In this current place where you find yourself, take what you see in your experiences and commit to looking in. Seek to find and access the truth that lives within you, to build awareness, engagement and finally ownership of who you are for the purpose of gifting YOU more fully into the world.

If you are ready to embrace the process of waking up and learn how to be more intentional, courageous and sovereign in how you lead and live, then let's get started!

INTERLUDE

Soul Role vs. the Conditioned Identity: Living a Leased Life?

"These are the roles and behaviors that many of us were raised to adopt, even if they don't reflect who we are deep down inside ... a fear of being perceived as weak forces men into pretending they are never afraid, lonely, confused, vulnerable or wrong; and extreme fear of being perceived as cold-hearted, imperfect, high maintenance or difficult forces women to pretend they're never exhausted, ambitious, pissed off or even hungry."

—Brené Brown

I LOVE THIS BRENÉ BROWN QUOTE. I do believe, too, that it really only scratches the surface.

The question I'd like to pose is this, are you living a borrowed or leased life? Are you thinking, reacting and making choices based on what you've seen others do, what others think and what you might have been raised to believe you are to do, be, have and want?

Or, on the other hand, do you OWN your life choices, non-dependent upon whether or not others agree or find who you are and what you do acceptable?

From the moment we are born, the conditioning begins. We are trained to "do" in order to "be." "Do this and you can Be that." "Act this way and you can belong and will be loved." "Take these classes and get good grades and you can be a success."

It shows up everywhere. In school, we are taught to follow the leader and fit into the norms of what can be categorized, organized, measured and controlled. Even when we discover greatness of our own that is unique, we are asked and expected to act and be a certain way. "Stay humble, don't think too highly of yourself," as if, somehow, feeling special and enjoying our individual gifts, simply for the experience of it, makes us egoic and separates us, in a negative way, from the rest.

On the other side, we might be told we must use our special talents to increase our own advantage and the success of others — that it is our "duty" and "responsibility" to USE our greatness for good. Then we are asked to drill down on this brilliance and create something that we can trade in for success and glory — something upon which we can capitalize.

I experienced this when I was a kid. I was an extraordinarily gifted swimmer. By the age of nine, I already had coaches looking at me for possible Junior Olympic training potential. The thing was, I simply loved swimming. Not to win, which I did, but to experience how great it felt to push my body to top levels of speed and precision. I didn't do it for the recognition, in fact, I was often MIA when it came time to receive my awards.

The older I got the more the adults in my life — thankfully, not my parents — wanted to use this talent to raise my team and eventually me to a place of top billing — success and all that came with it. Eventually, the pressure made me stop enjoying what I was doing. My life had become endless practices, and there was never time for friends. I decided, at the age of 12, to leave swimming so that I could have a life.

It is no wonder, with so much conditioning around our identities, that many are afraid to look in and uncover and define, for themselves, their distinct value. I know I felt like that much of my life. After the swimming experience, I was almost afraid to show what I was good at, lest someone come along and try to control how I use my skills and to what end.

We have been so accustomed to listening to others to determine who, what and why we are, that it seems scary to think that, perhaps, we might hold very different information within us.

What if we find that what is inside contradicts what we have come to believe about ourselves and others? That could be a very heavy realization that we may be tempted not to endure.

Yet, when we don't, what then? Whether we are consciously aware of it or not, who we are and why we came will bleed through. If we are living a false life, in any way, it will show up in how we feel and what manifests in our lives.

We've all heard stories where success and having everything the world has promised will bring satisfaction, in fact, does not. Perhaps, we have even experienced this ourselves. Illusive happiness or lack of fulfillment comes from a place of living inauthentically. We may, in fact, be "doing" everything to create the accomplishment, advancement and prosperity we've been led to believe is the value we want, the value we're meant to have and be, but our "being" does not feel complete or aligned. Our life, in some way or all ways, may look good on paper, but, in reality, something isn't adding up.

It is in this awareness where the opportunity is granted for us to see that we are not here to find out what the world wants from us. Instead, it is our soul's right and duty to determine what we've been carrying since birth that is the value we have to offer the world.

So, ask yourself: Are you truly ready to dive into the practice of discovering who you are, what you're made of and then becoming unapologetic about it?

If not, are you rightfully in a position to effectively lead?

If so, then it's vitally important that you understand the difference between a Soul choice, and one based on a

Role you think you are to play.

It's also important to know that what you find may have you questioning quite a bit. The discomfort that comes with this is a necessary part of the process of shifting from a conditioned state to a sovereign one.

Life is like a play where we hold multiple roles that we are asked to enact, simultaneously. We learn to identify our very being by these roles, and we are told that playing them to the greatest and highest degree of our capacity IS our personal value.

But, what if it has never been about the roles at all? What if we were to strip ourselves of these hats and titles? What would we be then?

If I were to ask the question of myself, "Who am I?" and I couldn't answer a daughter, sister, wife, mother, coach, writer, speaker or even woman, what would I say?

Who are YOU?

As Eric Greitens writes in his book *Resilience*, "To make the world excellent, great and beautiful, we may have to be a little irrational, a bit strange and sometimes odd." In other words, we may just need to be who we were born to be.

One of the things I like to suggest when facing the question "Who am I?" is this: Consider what purpose you have in life. Why do you think you were brought here at this time in history to have this particular life experience? To add value and impact?

To stimulate this thought process, ask yourself what others have said about you, good and bad, that has surprised you over the years.

For me, I have often been told I think too much and ask too many questions — that I should stop being so hard on myself when I go digging into understanding why I act, think and perceive things a certain way. I have also been told I am incredibly wise and have an extraordinary talent for reading people.

Quite frankly, before I began my coaching career, some of the things I was told about myself both surprised and shamed me. When it came to a few significant traits I had been told I had, I felt wrong or different and didn't really understand why and what I was supposed to do about it. I couldn't really grasp why others had these opinions of me; after all, I was just being me and didn't really want to think much about why or if that was good or bad. I knew, early on, that being judged didn't feel good.

What I have come to know and honor now is that I am a truth seeker. Self-inquiry is my game! I was created to ask a lot of questions, dig for meaning and have the ability to read people. My service to the world is to help others see their inner brilliance and bridge the gap between living a life that doesn't feel quite right to embracing who and what they were created to be.

So, I challenge you to really think about this. What is your ultimate role in life?

Your soul role.

We struggle with answering this question because we've been conditioned to fit into societal and familial norms. We've learned that to name it, categorize it and stick it in a box is to know it. And God help us if we don't know it! All hell breaks loose when we cannot be certain of things, right?!

We have become all about cerebral knowing, for sure! But what of instinctive knowing? Heart knowing? Soul knowing?

Now, don't get me wrong, there is certainly room for head-based thinking. Just not, in my humble opinion, when it comes to defining the fundamental question of who we are.

We have difficulty answering the question, "Who am I?" because we've been trained to think with our heads and not with our hearts and from our instinctive centers.

In his article, *The 4 Most Important (and Rare) Leadership Skills We Need for Our Future*, Shane Snow, award-winning entrepreneur, explorer, journalist and author of the #1 business bestseller *Dream Teams* talks about the huge changes that were ushered in by 2020 and what this has taught us about leadership:

"Gone are the days when the leaders that made sense for humanity were 'the big guy who fights good.' And gone are the days when it was smart to pick 'the guy who says he has all the answers.'

"Those kinds of 'linchpin' leaders are fallible because they're human. And these days they're an enormous risk. Because when they're wrong, or when their 'strength' manifests as stubbornness, the results can be devastating.

"When people disagree with them, too many traditional leaders dig in, shut out, or otherwise react shortsightedly."

In other words, leaders need to know and own themselves from a place of inner truth to be and act from a place of grounded authenticity, rather than ego and conditioning.

Another of my favorite quotes by Eric Greitens is "Great changes come when we make small adjustments with great conviction."

The word that stands out for me is *conviction*. I believe it's a powerful word with the potential to shift how we perceive and do things.

Depending on where you look for the meaning, the word "conviction" is defined as a few things, one being an article of faith.

Faith . . . another very powerful word!

So, if you are still having a tough time coming up with surprising things shared by others about you, start with a list of convictions. What are areas in your life where you have deep faith that something is true? This list will begin to give you the building blocks needed to define who you are.

This exercise is a bit tricky. If you are doing it properly, most of what ends up on that list is not something that can be tested or proven externally. In other words, you will be challenged to find hard, cold, factual and physical proof that your convictions are indeed true. What you will call on in creating this list is how you feel, what you sense and trust to be real.

For instance, I would say that my mother loves me, and as a sign of "proof," I could show her acts of kindness and words of love over the many years she raised me. In reality, however, that isn't physical proof at all. What if my mother had been solely acting from a place of obligation? What if she just said she loved me, but really didn't? The point is, I know my mother loves me, not based on anything I can measure, but based on how I feel, what I sense to be true and what I trust to be real. In other words, because I have faith that she does.

Okay, back to the question, WHO AM I? Hopefully, you can see now that this, too, is not a question we can answer truthfully from a place of conditioned, external information. We must dig into our soul to retrieve our authentic meaning.

Why is this necessary? Well, because we were created to know what service we are here to perform. I mean, think about it, how could you even begin to see to your duties at work if you didn't have a job description? If you didn't know your title and what was expected of you, how would you know what to do? You would end up wandering around the office looking for your place and not feeling like you were really getting much done, being very purposeful or even fitting in.

How many of us are living our lives this way, not knowing who we truly are or how we are meant to authentically serve? We may be comfortably numb, but are we truly living?

I don't believe any of us came into this life to play small, but in order to take our rightful place, we need to know what it is.

So, trust me, it's worth it to take the time to ask these questions. The true meaning of your unique life depends on it.

My question for you is this: Are you ready to stop leasing your life and OWN it?

If so, let the journey begin!

ACT 1

Building Awareness: A Discovery of Imposter Syndrome and the 3 Zones

"The path to becoming your own conscious leader will be different from the path of others, but every path shares several core elements. One of these is the vital role that questions — mostly inside questions — will play in your journey of self-discovery, self-awareness and self-truth. Critically, you must be willing to tell yourself the truth and to seek others who will help you see your own truth. This is the way of the conscious leader."

—Jeff Nischwitz

WE ALL PLAY THE PART OF CHIEF, IN SOME WAY. To legitimize our sense of "rightfulness" within this and every "role" we personate in life, discovering our innate leadership model is essential. It starts with fully uncovering, defining and owning who we truly are and what our purpose and mission are within this lifetime.

Without doing this, it is far too easy to be rocked off our chosen path by the conditioned values and expectations of others. This leaves us living a life that is far from genuine and that, oftentimes, has us feeling like a fraud.

In 1978, psychologists Pauline Rose Clance and Suzanne Imes coined the term *imposter phenomenon* to describe the belief that success comes by chance and is not due to talent or qualifications. People suffering from this condition experience feelings of not being good enough, despite merits and demonstrations of traditionally measured success. They undergo relentless episodes of self-doubt and question their abilities to the point of nullifying their actual achievements and capabilities.

Now commonly known as *imposter syndrome*, the current estimate is that, at some point, 70 percent of us experience a sense of complete disconnect from what we have come to understand as our abilities and competencies. This has us feeling a sense of "fakeness" and inadequacy.

My question is: What if when we encounter the belief that we are not equal to our success and earnings, it is not about disqualifying who we actually are, but who and how we've been led to categorize and evaluate ourselves to be?

What if imposter syndrome is an awakening to our genuine value?

Could what we have been seeing as a "breakdown" of belief in self actually be a dissolution of the method and system by which we rate and appraise who and what we are? What if it is meant to help us "declutter" and sift out what is true and what is conditioning?

If I wanted to renovate and reorganize a space in my home that is jam-packed with stuff, I would first have to clear out the clutter. I would need to take out, sort through and question what stays and what goes. I would have to clear the space completely, so that I could see that with which I have to work — the true value of the space.

What if that is exactly what imposter syndrome is attempting to do for people experiencing it? Perhaps, it's a removal of what doesn't belong to find what does.

We could also use the detox analogy. If you have ever done a body detox, you know you tend to feel much worse before you feel better. This is because, as the toxins you are expelling come up and out, you are meant to feel them, partially, so that you don't want to put them back in. The experience makes you aware of what is "good" and what compromises the effective and sustained functioning of the body system.

The symptoms of imposter syndrome run the gamut, but I gather that none of them feel good. Here are some that have been cited in a recent article by Zencare.

- Extreme lack of self-confidence
- Feelings of inadequacy
- Constant comparison to other people
- Anxiety
- Self-doubt
- Distrust in one's own intuition and capabilities
- Negative self-talk
- Dwelling on the past
- Irrational fears of the future

If you look closely at these and consider them in terms of how we are typically conditioned to think and behave, then you can see what I am saying.

Our world constantly feeds us messages about how we are to compare ourselves to a particular "scale" of success, that we need to learn from what has been done in the past, and that we should fear what is unknown in the future. On top of this, we are taught not to trust what we think, believe or sense, ourselves, but, instead, to follow, without question, what the "experts" and trusted studies and science say about what will help, support and be right for us.

Could it be that what we call symptoms of imposter syndrome are caused by the colliding of years of heavy influencing with that part of us, buried deep inside, that knows differently?

The simple fact that people experiencing imposter syndrome aren't able to evaluate themselves by the classic definitions of recognition, accomplishment and advancement has me wondering if, perhaps, this "syndrome" is actually the undoing of the illusionary expectations that we have been acculturated to believe and adopt. What if the feelings of being an "imposter" are a casting off, not of our true, innate Zone of Brilliance and value, but of the habituated way in which we have been taught to look at and determine our gifts and capacities, in addition to what constitutes the right way for us to "show up" in the world?

What if the true imposter is the traditional assessment of success and value — the visible "doings," merits, achievements, credentials and certifications, as well as the need to regulate, with concrete proof, that which has been developed as a valuation by the outside world?

What I present for consideration is that, after centuries of focus on the wrong qualifications, imposter syndrome, like most afflictions, ailments, disorders, crises and imbalances, is an indication of something far deeper. In this case, it's a sign of the improper evaluation of our true value and how we are to share it in this world.

Looking at imposter syndrome as the canary in the coal mine shows us that, perhaps, the condition is attempting to illuminate how misled and out of alignment we have been in our categorizations and appraisals. Seeing that it is possible people experiencing this syndrome are trying to free themselves from an antiquated analysis of and approach to recognizing and intentionally applying who they came to be and how they came to measure and deliver their talents and gifts allows us to view this issue in a whole new light.

If evolution is a way to bring about necessary change, balance and advancement, what if we are, collectively, in a time when the practice of judging ourselves based on a false measurement of success is being revealed? What if this indicates a new pattern in civilization that reflects a readiness to align with our unique identities in order to allow ourselves to show up, fully, in sovereign self-expression and empowerment?

In this world where we are quick to diagnose something as a malady, we might want to step back and look at imposter syndrome as a type of potential healing, instead.

Perhaps, the driving force that shows up as anxiety in people with imposter syndrome is actually about wanting to be seen, heard, understood and valued, not for what they can produce, but, in fact, for simply who they are.

I remember feeling all of this when I was in my mid-thirties and trying to have a child. Our culture has us approaching the struggle to conceive as a disease. We call it infertility, even before we have tested our bodies to determine if everything is, in fact, in working order. We immediately judge the inability to "produce" as proof of a problem with ourselves, as well as a need to measure and "fix" the situation, which first begins by labeling it.

I remember, as if it were yesterday, sitting down in a swanky office across from the top infertility doctor at one of the leading hospitals in this country. My OB/GYN was friendly with him, so he had fit me in.

Shuffling the papers in front of him, the doctor took a few moments to collect his thoughts. There was an uncomfortable silence. Finally, he leaned forward, looking down at my test results, and over the top of his glasses informed me, "We have identified and diagnosed the reason for your infertility."

He paused. I waited. Then, he finally said, "It's unexplained infertility."

I remember literally holding myself back from laughing out loud. I can only imagine the look on my face.

"So, let me make sure I understand this," I said very slowly. "Your 'diagnosis' is that you don't know why I can't conceive?"

The doctor furrowed his brow and looked visibly uncomfortable. He cleared his throat and replied, "All of your tests indicate that from a functional standpoint, everything is in working order."

I responded, "That is great news, but I'm still confused about how this constitutes a diagnosis?"

The doctor went on as if I had said nothing, "Due to your advanced maternal aging, we recommend in vitro fertilization."

"I'm only 36," I thought to myself. I also had enough knowledge about health and human biology that I knew there was a lot that didn't add up. I looked at him, incredulously.

"Okay," I said, looking directly across his massive walnut desk. "I don't want to seem disrespectful, but what you are proposing doesn't make any sense to me. You're telling me there doesn't seem to be any reason you can find that, from a physical standpoint, I cannot get pregnant, but you want me to immediately, because of my age, invest thousands of dollars to inject synthetic hormones into my body, hoping that this will 'cure' whatever natural imbalance I have, so I can get pregnant?"

The doctor sighed and took a deep breath. "Mrs. Philips, I am here to give you my professional opinion. What you do with it is entirely up to you."

I looked at him, smiling, "I appreciate that and would like to know your opinion on addressing my nutrition and seeking ways to balance my system naturally. Is it possible my issue is a deficiency in key nutrients or a need to detox in some way?"

The doctor stared back at me as if I had just spoken in a foreign tongue. He didn't blink and responded very slowly, as if speaking to a two-year-old. "In my opinion, that would be a waste of your time, but you could always try that approach if the in vitro doesn't work."

At that, I looked around the room, noticing all the certifications and credentials decorating the walls. I stood up, politely thanked the doctor and walked out of his prestigious office.

I believe our culture suffers from a disconnect with ourselves. We are so quick to listen to the counsel of others that we have stopped listening to our own inner adviser. There is a happy ending to my "infertility" story. I listened to my own guidance and hired a nutritionist and acupuncturist who helped me improve my health and create a more conducive environment for a potential child to come into. It worked, and within eight months, I conceived! I also enjoyed a blissful pregnancy, had tons of energy, no morning sickness and delivered a full-term baby girl.

The point of telling this story is to illustrate the importance of aligning with what is true for you, and not allowing outside measurements of what will bring success or failure to impede you from creating your own lane in which to navigate life. None of us are here to be evaluated by our success or lack of it. Instead, we get to be measured by our ability to be congruent within ourselves and make an impact from our unique Zones of Brilliance and Achievement. Only from this place will we have the opportunity to serve at our greatest potential.

THE 3 ZONES

I first began thinking about the concept of zones when I read Gay Hendricks' book *The Big Leap,* but the idea for the 3 Zones came to me a couple of years ago after a discussion with my client, Paul, (name has been changed for confidentiality) about how to use my WHAT-HOW-WHERE model as a tool to create a "lane" for himself. As I explained to him, staying in your lane permits you to serve from your innate gifts in a way that is naturally in tune with how you desire to be and within the boundaries that are set around what best supports and nourishes you.

The Importance of Staying in Your Lane

A number of years ago, I had the opportunity to visit Paris with my family. The second day in the City of Lights, we visited the Arc de Triomphe. Looking down from the top of the Arch, you get an amazing view of the city, the grand avenue, Champs-Élysées, and the other 11 avenues that form the étoile (star) at the center of which sits the Arch.

You also get a great view of the "bumper car" – like display of motorcycles, buses, cars and, yes, even bicycles making their way around what looks like it would probably be a four-lane roadway that encircles the Arch. To the American eye, it looks like pure chaos.

Upon looking down at all this, my 10-year-old daughter furrowed her brow. "Why don't they have any lanes?" she asked. "They look like they're all going to run into one another!"

And it was true, not to mention incredibly amusing to watch.

Apparently, "the traffic circle at the Arc de Triomphe is the only place in Paris where accidents are not judged. No matter what the circumstances, insurance companies split the costs 50-50," wrote Rick Steves in his article, "Circling In On Paris' Arc de Triomphe."

This brings up an interesting observation: It makes sense not to have lanes if there isn't going to be any accountability for personal responsibility. There is a reason the term "laissez faire" comes from the French, perhaps, yet it becomes even more apparent to me the importance of lanes and why they do exist, to begin with. Without them, it seems that "live and let live" cannot truly work the way in which it's meant.

Could you imagine bowling, driving on the highway or checking out at the grocery store without lanes? It would look and feel like, well ... driving in the traffic circle at the Arc de Triomphe! Funny to watch, but not so much fun or efficient from the point of view of the people involved.

One of the reasons seeing the chaotic traffic patterns at the Arc de Triomphe hit such a cord for me is that, over the years, I have found myself in conversation after conversation with clients where the importance of "staying in your own lane" has come up.

It first surfaced in a session with a client who was expressing concern over his pattern of, as he put it, "doing too much and then feeling anxious."

I asked if the moments of "doing too much" constituted focusing on things that were in his own lane.

"What do you mean, 'in my own lane'?" he asked.

"I find that anxiety emerges when we are doing things out of our lane," I replied. "Things that are really someone else's responsibility. The anxiety is a signal that we have veered out of our lane and into someone else's."

"Hmm," he responded, simply.

"I believe we all came to our individual lives to experience and learn. Our independent life journeys are our way to have lessons and grow. If each path is a 'lane,' it's easier to see why my driving into your lane can disrupt your ability to experience the things and have the lessons you came here to have. It also keeps me from having the ones in my own lane that I came here to encounter."

"So, what about our interactions with others and helping?" my client inquired.

"It depends on your intent," I said. "It is possible to supportively interact with others without leaving your own lane. It's when you are rescuing, trying to fix or control another or the circumstances in their lane that you have exited yours. I believe we are all creators of our own lives. We are here to take full responsibility for what is going on in our lanes. We can certainly ask for support, guidance and positive reinforcement from others, but it depends on our intention whether or not we are taking the responsibility ourselves or trying to get other people to leave their lanes to fix something in ours."

I continue to have conversations about this "lane" concept. This tells me it's a pattern coming up for many of us.

Taking mature responsibility for our lives means seeing ourselves as creators, not as victims, perpetrators or saviors. We manifest what we experience. Attending to what is in our own lane, while allowing others to do the same, IS the most loving and mature thing to do.

As you consider this piece within your own life and your desire to be your own creator, it's helpful to think about patterns from the past, especially around putting others ahead of your own self-love and nurturance. This also applies to you expecting others to put you ahead of theirs.

How can you become more mindful of the practice of "staying in your own lane"? Consider the impact of being the rescuer or the victim who either takes on the full responsibility of another's physical and emotional well-being or expects another to do this for you. Have you experienced a sense of obligation or "duty" about something and felt resentful about it? This could be because you are out of your lane doing something that is not your responsibility instead of allowing yourself to experience and choose action from a place of desired support.

Now contemplate being the mature creator who steps up to take complete responsibility for their own life and desires. Or the supporter for others who is there to share information and themselves as an energetic space-holder, allowing others the place and opportunity to be responsible for making it okay physically and emotionally for themselves.

What does each consideration feel like to you? What new insights can you get from this?

We all get overwhelmed from time to time. Remember that when a moment "seems too much," we have the opportunity to see that we have been stepping outside of our lane of responsibility or have been asking another to do this for us. In these moments, we can compassionately redirect ourselves back into our own lane and communicate whatever is necessary to correct our overstepping.

Understanding the concept of "lane" allows us to begin to see the relevance of "zone," as well. For me, knowing I need to stay in my own lane is step 1. Defining what that "lane" is for me and its boundaries constitutes my understanding and ownership of a zone.

Upon hearing me talk about the importance of staying in one's own "lane," Paul, who had had some amateur race car driving experience, shared The Zone Control System, which, in racing, is a method comprising six zones of space surrounding a vehicle. Using the Zone Control approach allows a driver to effectively respond to any variations within the driving environment by remaining in control of the vehicle, thus making the best possible decisions and producing the greatest potential outcome.

This stimulated my own thoughts about designing a tool for my clients that would enable them to remember and align with their truth, power and personal locus of control, as well as know how they can create, live and lead from this central place of command. A number of weeks later, I was interviewed on the podcast *Girls Who Do Stuff* by my friends, Jenny Midgley and Sarah Madras. I spoke about the importance of "Owning Your Zone." Jenny immediately said there was something there that I needed to unpack and create. From there, the following model was born.

ZONE 1 : THE ZONE OF BRILLIANCE

In the WHAT-HOW-WHERE model,
this is the WHAT.
It's who we were born to be. Our *innate* value.

Our Zone of Brilliance (ZOB) is made up of all of our natural-born traits, talents, gifts and aptitudes. These are the inherent abilities we have both intentionally honed and the ones that might still be latent within us. All of them were bestowed upon us before we came into this world as the primary ways in which we are meant to create, develop, support and bring something unique and special to the world.

When I was a kid, I was often told that I was a "troublemaker." I remember actually being surprised and confused by this remark or scolding. The times it happened, I was simply sharing an observance or acting upon a situation that didn't appear right or just to me. In these occasions, as I later recognized through unpacking and studying the situational facts and motives, what was causing me to speak or act up was an ability to read and translate cues and patterns that spoke to incongruencies and "gaps" in other people's language and actions.

In other words, I could hear and see where people were withholding information, not telling the truth and attempting to control the situation, in some way. I would respond with questions or comments directly targeting the "missing" information and calling attention to what I had observed. In this way, I found myself "in trouble" for highlighting something the other person didn't want to address, have scrutinized or have to explain.

My ability to detect cues in other's verbal and non-verbal language was (and still is) an innate trait. In developing my awareness of this and seeing where it has value, I now appreciate this as a gift. It is the primary skill that I use to help my clients discover, define and own their own inherent values and gifts.

ZONE 2: THE ZONE OF ACHIEVEMENT

This is HOW we have navigated and adapted our inner brilliance to outer world experiences and conditioning. It comprises our acquired skills and competencies. The things we have learned to do and be. Our *earned* value.

We see our Zone of Achievement (ZOA) show up in résumés, career titles and lists of merits, credentials and certifications of expertise. We are trained to identify this zone as our primary value in life and to work hard to hone and build it. We are taught it is through our achievements and subsequent learned skills that we are to serve the world.

Similarly, we have attached monetary value to this zone. We have been told that if we "work hard and achieve much, we will be properly rewarded." We have been shown that we must strive for our value and produce something valuable to be someone valuable. We have been conditioned to believe that to "be valuable and valued in life," we must apply consistent effort, grit, drive and sacrificial practice.

Yet, when it comes to authentic value, I have found that the attachment of self-identification to this acculturated model is what has kept many of us from being able to actually fully and freely deliver our true gifts and talents. While I do believe that our ZOA is important and a big part of what we came here to experience and from which to learn and grow, I find it is our ZOB that is the coveted offering through which we came to serve and deliver our primary value. Our ZOA is what we are meant to use to support our ZOB.

Let's look at this for a moment through the lens of what I call "Grounding In to Level Up."

One of the things I enjoy about my work is the ability to speak with enough people about the foundational shifts going on in their lives to see collective patterns and trends that run through each of their stories.

A big one that has had a great influence on my work is what I call the "Need to Come Home." The way I explain this is a timely development that arises within an individual and stems from many years of conditioning and practice around "grounding" themselves to outside sources.

We used to call this the "midlife crisis," but more recently with terms like "quarter-life crisis" and the "crises" that appear earlier and earlier in our collective youth populations, I don't think this development is a "midlife" issue alone. The need to ground ourselves is not a new awareness, as much as it seems to be a new and significant need for people to understand and find this place of home NOW to prepare for the way the world is currently evolving and to connect with who they are and where they fit in the bigger puzzle of life.

Through the practice of grounding externally, people come to believe that if and when they have this grade, acknowledgment, job/career, relationship or amount of money in the bank, then they will feel safe and secure.

This has always been an illusionary goal. These are the things we cannot control in life when it comes to protecting them from the influence of change. In other words, we can get the A and still fail the class. We can have more than a million followers on social media and lose our status overnight. We can be offered the job and then lose it. We can build the successful career and then something can happen to take it all away. We can have the relationship that changes and fades, and the money, well, we know that can go in the blink of an eye.

Spiritual teacher Todd Savvas puts it this way:

"It's about feeling settled and in the right place. External elements always shift and change, so your foundation can't truly be reliant on those factors. The only place to find true foundation and groundedness is within, which is about your relationship with your soul or truest self. The only way to feel authentic inner contentment is to work on making YOURSELF your home, your rock, your safe place. From here, everything surrounding you will align."

A current statistic is that more than 40 million Americans suffer from anxiety. I believe this stress arises from a deep, overwhelming fear of not being safe and secure.

So many of us are out there operating from an inner drive to HAVE in order to BE. Telling ourselves, "I must have this thing to be safe, happy, fulfilled, enough ..."

The biggest problem, other than the constant change that affects what we are chasing, is that this belief is fundamentally untrue.

We don't need to HAVE anything to BE who we were made to be, which is inherently valuable, and truly understanding this becomes our security.

Right here, in this moment, we are now being. It is the traits within this being that we are meant to bring forward, develop, define and see as our value. We are also meant to secure ourselves to the significance of this value, our ZOB.

Look at it this way, I'm still BEING, even without a job or career or relationship or money. When we use language that suggests otherwise, we are operating from an illusionary state.

So, my question is not "what do you need to feel grounded and secure in life," but rather, "how do you need to be for groundedness and security to be your reality?"

Here are a few areas where you can begin creating skills (ZOA) that will allow for a stronger and more grounded sense of self (the foundation for building awareness and definition of your ZOB):

- **Build trust** – When you don't trust who you are and how you operate, you are going to have a hard time grounding within to find a sense of safety and security. Building trust starts with being honest with yourself about everything you hold within you. It then involves aligning your truths with approaches to handling them and being that are in integrity with who you are.

- **Be aware and present** – When you are always looking for that "next fix" to distract yourself from your own thoughts, feelings and inner voice, you will not be able to know, connect with or own your true self.

- **Practice neutral observation** – We all bring our "stories" to the table, which can keep us functioning from a state of illusion and reaction instead of from a place of being with "what is." You notice a whole lot more about yourself and others when you learn to separate what's yours from the experiences of the present moment.

- **Listen to and honor your gut and how you feel –** This is not about the emotions that arise from a triggered state. Acknowledging and having reverence for your heart and gut in "neutral" moments allows you to act from a place of discernment and not from an eventual state of judgment or criticism, which is always about choice to be with something that is misaligned with you.

One of the most important things for me, as I support the identity and performance of my clients, is the alignment of true self and mission. You cannot know what you are truly here for if you don't first identify who you are, what you offer and what you honestly need to sustain yourself.

To level up in life, whether that be to break through a conditioned and self-imposed ceiling, evolve as a person or become a more enlightened leader, the first step is to come home and build a solid state of knowing that who you are is who you want to be and what you create in everything you think, say and do IS your legacy in the time you're here.

As you begin to look at your areas of brilliance and achievement differently, where can you start to place the skills and what you have learned in the position of support for the natural genius that lies within you? Instead of viewing your ZOA as your primary value, and identifying yourself through this zone, how can you begin to pick out the importance of your learned expertise, as it applies to HOW you show up and deliver within your ZOB?

ZONE **3**: THE ZONE OF IMPACT

*If Who We Are Here to Be is our **Zone of Brilliance**, and our **Zone of Achievement** is How We Are Here to Be, then Why We Are Here, or our mission and purpose, is our **Zone of Impact**.*

> **Zone of Brilliance + Zone of Achievement = Zone of Impact**

One of my roles, when working with my visionary clients, is to help them assemble their teams. Once a visionary defines and truly understands their Zone of Impact (ZOI), what they can achieve if they adhere to the boundaries of their "lane," they become painfully aware of what happens when they try to leave this lane. They begin to see just how important it is to find others to fill the necessary roles within the company and how essential it is to choose people whose own ZOB, ZOA and ZOI align to the seat or "lane" from which they are hired to operate.

In the book *Rocket Fuel*, Entrepreneurial Operating System inventor Gino Wickman and his business partner Mark C. Winters discuss the vital relationship of the visionary and integrator. They go to lengths to describe the unique roles and traits of each and how one without the other results in a system that simply cannot thrive.

Famous V/I teams in history have been Walt Disney and his brother, Roy Disney, as well as Warren Buffett and Charlie Munger and Steve Jobs and Steve Wozniak.

We can use this model of visionary/integrator to define our Zone of Brilliance and our Zone of Achievement, as well. Our ZOB comprises all of the innate gifts that reflect WHAT we are here to bring to the world. Our ZOA is made up of the acquired and earned skill sets that determine HOW we are to deliver our inherent value forward. Our own internal V/I team of ZOB and ZOA, therefore, allows us to create the impact and Legacy that we are designed to effectuate.

When we have a clearly defined understanding of both our ZOB and our ZOA, we can see where one is not more or less important than the other when it comes to our ZOI (Legacy). We can honor and apply each where it belongs and where its role is most warranted. This makes room for a collaborative effort, within ourselves, where both our ZOB and ZOA are celebrated and supported to make an impact within the space that was uniquely created for it. With this model, there is no more need for inner struggles (Be Myself vs. Successfully Produce or Do What I Love vs. Make a "Living") or for suffering from imposter syndrome. Within this framework, we can see the value of all of our zones for the impact each makes in the creation of our overall life experiences and legacy.

I have witnessed that we struggle to see our different zones of value and also to operate successfully within them to produce the legacy we know, deep down, we are meant to deliver. I believe in the polarized world in which we have lived, one of the reasons for this is, we have been taught to manage our suffering instead of empowering our value.

The age-old paradigm of suffering has us working

from a disempowered dynamic which has us either living from a mentality of victimization (what we aren't, cannot do and cannot achieve) or from a position of perpetuating it.

The model of managing suffering creates the need for competition, which breeds a "right or wrong" approach to living and supports the need for polarization and dichotomous thinking. Here, you are winning or losing, functioning or broken. You're either "with us or against us."

When we begin to shift to a model of empowering value, we are invited to look through the lens of creator, where we recognize our power to manifest everything we experience. We progress through the process of building awareness of our value to engaging with this value to better develop and understand it, and finally to owning our value, so that we have the confidence, clarity and acceptance of how our value is not only valuable, but meant to be valued.

The model of empowering value takes away any need for competition, because we are all focused on finding just where our own unique value can augment that of the collective whole. We strive to bring the best version of our value forward. That challenge to grow and develop ourselves becomes our driving force. This paradigm creates a natural necessity for collaboration, advances our understanding of "together we are better," and has us looking for the win-win solution.

In Act 1, we have taken time to build awareness of your personal "lane" and why it's important to define it. We've discussed and dissected imposter syndrome and what constitutes your lane — your 3 Zones. Next, you'll learn to discover how to define your own zones and how this helps you better understand who you are and how you can best approach your unique brand of leadership and live your life more fully and authentically.

ACT 2

Seeking Engagement:
Creating Our Inner Leadership Model
through Defining Our 3 Zones

"Freedom is on the other side of reflection. As difficult as it may be to disengage from attachments and co-dependencies, the freedom to become more authentic and sovereign in your life is worth what you are being asked to give up. Be aware of your insights, intuition and curiosity. Use what you see to question everything and discern what makes sense internally for you. Be inspired by the answers and what you are coming to realize and know."

—Lena Stevens

Throughout history, we have learned to fight. We fight for what we want. We fight against what we don't want. We have often played on the defensive team, blocking and tackling what life brings to our doors. We've been on autopilot and automatic. We've been reactive in our thoughts, interpretations and actions. And we have been desperate to find our own, internal leadership: the place where we feel confident, grounded and sure of who we are and what we are meant to do.

I believe when we find ourselves seeking, it's a cue that we are being given an incredible invitation and opportunity to do things differently. Perhaps, at this time in your life, the proposition is for you to be collaborative instead of competitive and resistant. To ask, of yourself, to BE better in order to DO better. To realize that even if you find yourself confused and uncomfortable, you can still approach others and situations from a place of curiosity, patience and compassion.

Whether it is in your personal or professional life, you CAN grow and you CAN rise above where you've gone, what you've done and who you've been. It takes awareness, dedication and ownership, not for others, but for yourself, first. You live in closest proximity to you. Therefore, liking who you are and how you show up in this world is essential. This is the only way you will stay accountable to being better to others. It comes from being better for yourself.

In learning about the 3 Zones, we have identified the importance and need to define Who We Are Innately (Zone of Brilliance), How We Are Meant to Apply Ourselves (Zone of Achievement) and What We Are Here to Experience and Leave Behind (Zone of Impact).

Once we have clarified what these are for us, the challenge is in showing up in our "lane," regardless of the environment in which we find ourselves and the difficulties we may endure.

The Importance of Words

In order to define anything, we need words. Words are very powerful, as we use them to give meaning and value to everything in life.

A 2013 study found the average woman uses 20,000 words a day, while the average man comes in at approximately 7,000 words.

The point here is not to dive into the reason for the number of words utilized by each gender, but to point out that words hold a tremendously important value in our lives.

We use words to communicate everything from the time of the day to life-or-death announcements. Because of this, as humans, we are wired to respond to the words we use and the words we receive from others.

How many times have we heard the expressions: "You're only as good as your word," "He's a man of his word" or "Be true to your word?"

If we are using and receiving so many words in a

given day, how intentional and aware are we about the power of these words?

We all know the Aesop's fable, The Boy Who Cried Wolf. The moral of the story is when we disrespect the power of words and our own integrity with the use of them, we lose our ability to be heard and seen for who we truly are.

When we aren't heard or seen, what does that say about our true connection with others? What does that say about us?

I believe one of the main reasons people struggle to show up, create and attend to goals and make the lives for themselves that they truly want is because they have so eroded their own level of self-trust. This happens after years of unmet promises that have resulted in an inability to trust one's own word.

Simply put, we have, too often, "cried wolf" in our own lives.

If we cannot trust ourselves, what does this mean for our capacity to trust others?

And what of the words that we use that don't adequately reflect what we truly feel and believe? How many times do we say (or don't say) things because we feel others expect them or would not approve if we communicated them?

What if there was something we gave our word to at an earlier time and things have authentically changed for us? How flexible and upstanding are we with being able to speak our new truth — our current word — even if it's not supported by our environment?

We can really see here how words, and our use of them, play such a huge role in our life expression and experience.

I feel we have witnessed a point of breakdown in

many areas when it comes to communicating our word. Perhaps, the best way to begin to get back to building faith, trust and legitimacy in our word is to focus on what it takes to do this.

First, it takes listening to our innate rumblings: the "messages" that come from deep within, calling us to create, express and be something.

I love what Lori Hamann says about life work, worth and our word:

"If you are not standing in your worth while you are doing 'that thing' called life's work, you aren't keeping your word to yourself and the world."

She goes on to add, "Your word is a powerful piece of the puzzle. It's your integrity. It has the power to make movement in your life and attract what you desire most, as a result."

In looking at this, we can see that where you feel "stuck" is where you have not been true to your word. Again, it's important to consider we are not talking about the word of others that stems from another's expectations of how things need to be, but from an authentic buy-in to your own life's purpose, direction and desires.

When you are "just doing as you are told," much of the time, you are not living by your own word.

It's very difficult to attend to the words that are not our own. Words that we have not owned because they do not reflect our truth, or because we have not taken the time to analyze and legitimize them for ourselves.

So, if we haven't "owned" them, why do we speak them? Why do we say something we know we can't/won't/will struggle to stand by?

And why don't we stand by the words we know are reflective of our truth?

It takes intention, presence, consistency and

commitment to take a good, long, hard look in the dermatological mirror. Seeing all that stuff close up can be very challenging.

Yet these are the questions that I feel we need to ask ourselves regarding the areas in our lives where we are most challenged when it comes to authorship and self-leadership.

The fact is, until we do, our word won't really mean much. We will continue to find ourselves in situations where both we and the people around us (acting as reflective mirrors) will continue to use words that are misrepresentative and lack substance.

Because, after all, if we are our word, then what does that say of us and of the lives we are living?

It's time to intentionally select the words we choose to live by.

DEFINING OUR 3 ZONES #1: THE ZONE OF BRILLIANCE

As mentioned previously, our Zone of Brilliance is who we were born to be and comprises our innate value traits.

The question that is answered by defining our Zone of Brilliance is: What am I here to be?

Our ability to verbalize our inherent value allows us to intentionally focus and deliver what we have to present and offer, simply by being who we are, and it creates more alignment and fulfillment in how we experience our engagements and how others experience us because it literally comes from the most authentic and genuine parts of ourselves.

As important as it is for Superman to know he can bend steel and fly, it is equally important that you are able to verbalize the value you bring to others — the value that IS you.

The process I use with clients to determine this value is below. We focus on individual words that we can then apply to any given situation to which we want to mindfully and meaningfully apply our innate value.

Defining Your Zone of Brilliance – The Process

- Make a list of all the words that describe you from a place of innate value. What have others told you about yourself over the years that might have surprised you? Think about traits that you might not have seen in yourself before they were mentioned to you.

- Then narrow down this list to your top five value words. These are the ones that BEST describe your value in the way it shows up in all aspects of your life and who you are.

- You can use your chosen words to complete the following statement: *"At my core, I am … and this is a gift I have to give at all times."* You can use this, in your day-to-day, to remind yourself of who you are and what you are here to offer to others and the experience in which you find yourself.

Discovering and Developing Our Inner Leadership Model: Consideration #1 – Engaging With Your Zone of Brilliance:

Now that you have your list of words that define WHO YOU ARE, as you begin to intentionally try them on for size, you might find yourself bumping up against behaviors that you have developed throughout your life that contradict this new value awareness that is emerging.

Since there are about as many reasons for this as there are different personalities and stories, one of the tools I like to use to discover key information is to look at the building blocks of self-worth/self-value.

Building Block #1: Awareness

In the beginning, we don't know what we don't know, right? Awareness is about revealing and identifying. It's about getting curious and asking the right questions to illuminate and test what's hidden beneath the surface of the self-identity we have come to know and believe that might be upsetting our ability to actually BE who we are.

Some great questions to start with are:

- What values are important to my family and those close to me? Are they different from any of my Zone of Brilliance words?

- What beliefs, moods, words, opinions, support, information, thoughts, ideas, etc., am I sharing with the world? How do I feel about this? Do these things align with my Zone of Brilliance words?

- What roles do I play in life and how am I showing up in these roles? Do I feel "successful" in these roles? Why or why not? How does this connect with my awareness of my Zone of Brilliance?

- Are there areas of my life that I see and feel are very congruent with my Zone of Brilliance and who I am intentionally applying myself to be? Are there areas that I see and feel are not aligned?

Building Block #2: Acceptance

Once we have begun to build some awareness around our value relationship, the next step is to empower it. If we don't accept who we are, how do we expect others to? Building acceptance of our Zone of Brilliance is about embracing and owning what we have to bring to the table, regardless of how this measures up with others or with how we have perceived our value in the past. It is crucial that we can share what we have to give to the world and have it show up powerfully and beneficially. Again, if Superman didn't know he could bend steel and fly, would he be in his full capacity to serve? Could others benefit as much from what he had to offer?

- What do you need to work on, release and accept about yourself to embrace and embody your Zone of Brilliance?

Building Block #3: Intention

I talk often about the difference between expectation and intention. Expectation is about the outside world and how I want it to show up for me. Intention is about the inner world and how I want to show up for myself, so that I can fully show up in and for the world. Intention is about setting a course. It's about knowing what and how we want our value to be in the world and making plans to put it there.

- What intentional statements can you make to support your Zone of Brilliance and allow it to show up fully in the world? Intentional Statements support your Goal Statements. They state how you choose to BE in order to do what you want to achieve and accomplish.

Building Block #4: Communication

Okay, so what is the point of having awareness, acceptance and intention if we aren't communicating our value to others? Many people believe that positive talk about oneself is akin to bragging, boasting or egoism. Of course, it depends on how you communicate what you have going for you. Knowing your gifts and being confident in speaking about what you have to give is best done with the intention to serve. When you regard it in this context, it becomes a matter of doing your duty and showing up to offer what you have, naturally, to bestow.

Similarly, if we are afraid to speak up about where we aren't being valued or if we cannot remove ourselves from situations where what we have to give is being squandered, then our gifts cannot be delivered where they will be best utilized. For these reasons, effective communication of what we know our value to be is crucial.

- Where and how do I observe myself communicating my Zone of Brilliance?

- Do I see patterns of self-deprecation or fear of speaking about my value? What may have caused this pattern?

- What story can I shift to in order to confidently see the importance of communicating what I have to offer so that others can benefit from it?

Building Block #5: Discernment

There is a big difference between judgment and discernment. Judgment is about our perception of something/someone not measuring up to certain standards. Discernment is about creating, upholding, believing and seeing to our personal standards within our own lives. It is about making sure we allow in what will support and protect our value. It is also about letting go of and not letting in what does not. We can do this without judgment. It simply becomes a question of what is needed and most fitting for us. This is where boundaries are important. It is crucial to know what best serves you and what is and is not okay for you. This is what allows you to protect, preserve, grow and practice your own, authentic value.

- Where might I be allowing influences, environments or other outside conditioning to affect how I show up in my Zone of Brilliance?

- How can I set more appropriate standards and boundaries around myself and my innate value?

Building Block #6: Commitment

If you interviewed successful individuals about the core values/practices that led to their growth and success, commitment would be at the top of that list. Commitment keeps us on course by allowing us to tap into our authentic passions and purpose. It is the dedication to showing up in our Zone of Brilliance no matter what and reaching for what it is we say we want and stand for the most.

- What can I commit to doing, today, that will keep me focused on delivering from my Zone of Brilliance so that I can ensure that I'm offering the best that I have to give, at all times?

Building Block #7: Trust and Faith

One of my favorite social meadia shares over the past few years is an illustration of Jesus kneeling down in front of a small child who is clinging to her prized possession, a very well-loved and worn teddy bear. In one hand, behind his back where the child cannot see, Jesus holds a much larger, new and beautiful teddy bear. With his other hand, he is reaching for the little bear that the child holds. The caption above his head reads: Trust me.

To allow for the flow of all things toward their desired and intended places, we must have trust and faith. This is a letting go and deep knowing that all will work out. It's a cognizance that if we have built the awareness, accepted, intentioned, communicated, practiced discernment and applied commitment, we have done all we can do.

The rest is up to what's left beyond c
control.

- Where can I make room fo'
  comes to allowing myself to i.
  Zone of Brilliance?

- Where can I develop faith that the situatio.
  experiencing is exactly what is called for, no ma.
  what it may look like on the surface?

- Where might there be a pattern of control that
  blocks me from doing this?

Keeping each of these building blocks in mind will
help to increase your awareness and the impact of your
innate value. Also, it will create a greater sense of purpose, which ultimately leads to experiencing more fulfillment in life.

#2: ZONE OF ACHIEVEMENT

In the way the world and society has developed, we have all been taught to build and hone the skills and talents within our Zone of Achievement. Again, as previously discussed, this zone is made up of our acquired, learned and earned strengths and abilities.

The question that is answered by defining our Zone of Achievement is: How am I here to be?

Your approach to life reflects how you choose to be. It's about how you decide to deliver the value you have to offer. The skills, abilities and behaviors that you have learned and acquired throughout life are your vehicle. They are there to facilitate and support the delivery of your Zone of Brilliance, and they constitute your approach to bringing these innate gifts to the table.

Similarly, if you have a particular approach to things that is not in alignment with your inherent value, it will be challenging for others to receive and benefit from what you have to give.

How you have been "trained" to be in your Zone of Achievement? Does it conflict with who you are authentically and how you are here to innately serve?

For three years, I worked with some federal prison

inmates who had been incarcerated for white collar crimes. Many had been successful businessmen and leaders in their professions. Almost all of them shared that who they dreamed of being when they were young boys was not what they ended up doing for a living. They had chosen careers that required impressive credentials and accumulated power and prestige, not because their inner being wanted it, but, for various reasons, because they felt that is who they needed to be to get what they wanted in life or to be something they were taught they were supposed to be. This disconnect with their Zone of Brilliance had them acting in ways that eventually landed them in a place of "do over" where they were given the opportunity to really think about how this disassociation from their natural gifts and desires had impacted their choices, behaviors, actions and outcomes.

We all have acquired useful talents and competencies that are highly advantageous. The key is to align them with our Zone of Brilliance and not tie our actual identity to them. They are here as support, not to personify who we are and what is truly valuable about us.

Defining Your Zone of Achievement – The Process

- List all the words that describe skills and behaviors you have learned that are valuable and helpful and that you intentionally want to use to support others.

For example, in my teaching and coaching careers, I learned to ask great questions to draw out the needs, values, intentions and goals of others. I want to help people connect with their potential so they can meet these needs, values, intentions and goals, so one of my approach words is "potentiating."

- Narrow your list down to the top five approach

words that you want to be intentional about in the future.

- You can use your chosen words to complete the following statement: *"At my core, my approach is … and this is how I wish to support others, at all times."* Work with these from a point of intention around how you wish to bring them to your day-to-day interactions and experiences.

Consider how you feel when you make these statements to yourself. What does it look like to show up this way? How do you get to think and see yourself to reflect these words to others? What does showing up in these ways inspire in others?

Discovering and Developing Our Inner Leadership Model: Consideration #2 – How Patterns of Belief Affect Our Zone of Achievement

If our Zone of Brilliance is WHAT we are in the world, our Zone of Achievement is HOW we choose to approach and apply ourselves in the world. It's also about HOW we want to be seen and interact with others. As mentioned, making sure our HOW is in alignment with our WHAT is essential to being recognized and experienced as the leader we are meant to be.

Sir Ernest Shackleton was a polar explorer who led three British expeditions to the Antarctic in the early 1900s. He was considered one of the principal figures of the period known as the Heroic Age of Antarctic Exploration.

A number of years ago, I read a story about his travel on The Endurance, the ship Shackleton and his crew sailed to take his Imperial Trans-Antarctic Expedition. During my reading, one thing kept coming up: the word "crisis."

When interviewed, Shackleton's crew stated there was no one they would rather have with them in crisis. This speaks to the fact that he was well-known in crisis situations; he was not new to them and had experienced his share, as documented in his many books that recounted his voyages and expeditions.

Which leads me to wonder, why?

Certainly, when we take big risks in life, there can be a greater chance for experiencing crisis. This does not always happen, however, unless we are wired with a belief system for it. If we believe, and, therefore, have an expectation that it is/will be a part of our experience, it is also highly possible that we will tend to believe that it is the way we can "prove" ourselves and define our value.

In this case, this "hero" approach to seeking out where we can "save the day" has us operating within our Zone of Achievement in such a way that can very well be creating or adding to the crisis itself.

I have worked with many leaders in some form of career crisis. What I find, over and over again as they talk of their experiences, is a belief that "this is just the way it is." Now, I have worked with people in many different industries, so I know, although what they are saying may be manifesting as "truth," the reason why they are experiencing things the way they are is that they perceive this is the way it's supposed to be.

Why do we do this?

Other than the typical sense perception that might dictate what we come to experience, a lot of why we are attracted to given situations is due to our beliefs.

What I find with many in places of high power and stressful industries is a practice of standard that goes like this:

If I lost my "fighting edge," I would no longer have the ability to make an impact.

We see this everywhere, but it's highly obvious in areas such as the military, the government and industries where big power is at play. The belief is that we must "fight" to show and prove our VALUE.

In addition, we have been wired and conditioned at every turn to believe we have to "expect the worst," and approach with "our guard up," "armed and ready."

We talk about the fight against inequality, the battle against cancer, the struggle to get ahead.

Our language is geared towards looking at and expecting crisis. The belief is getting our dukes up and guns ready means we are on alert and prepared for what's to come.

We see this when we talk of choosing procrastination because we perform better "under pressure."

What if it didn't have to be this way? What if preparation and performing at our best was more about the approach of being in the flow state of knowing and trusting in who we are and what we have to bring to the table? What if truly "being at our edge" is being present and focusing on what we have to offer (gifts, skill sets, etc.) so that when something does come down the pike, we are in a calm state of ready, and thus more apt to make a reasonable, quick and intuitive decision that leads us away from crisis instead of toward it. What if THIS state were considered "being the champion," "getting ahead" and "being prepared?"

What if serotonin trumped cortisol?

What if our vision of a hero was someone in a peaceful state of meditation instead of a combat soldier with bulging muscles and weaponry slung all over his body?

What if Shackleton (most likely subconsciously or

unconsciously) created crisis so that he could have the opportunity to perform "at his best"? The story narrative spoke to the fact that his expeditions were not as well planned and thought through as others of the time. It was common knowledge that he was known for rushing and jumping into things before the time was right and not adequately preparing. Is this truly something to celebrate?

Not to subtract from Shackleton's heroism, but if he had been more prepared and honored the needs of his men and himself, perhaps he wouldn't have needed to be a hero at all. Perhaps he had a belief that in order to have true value, he had to be the savior, so he created opportunities to be this.

I mention this because we have to watch what we believe in, follow and hold at high value. If it isn't in alignment with who we are and how we truly want to be, we need to consider shifting what we believe and subscribe to and how we look at the reality we experience.

When deciding anything, but especially how we align our Zone of Brilliance and our Zone of Achievement, if we don't fully understand our ultimate whys and the impact of what we choose to believe and from this, how we choose to act, we can be at risk of creating a reality that we (and others) don't want, thus risking the integrity of our personal leadership model.

#3: ZONE OF IMPACT

As mentioned previously, our Zone of Impact is about our purpose and mission. It's what we are meant to experience and create in this life. It speaks to our lessons, influence and the legacy we are to leave behind.

The question that is answered by defining our Zone of Impact is: Why am I here?

One of my core beliefs is that when I serve myself (needs, mission and purpose), all else is served. When I see to these things, everyone else gets what they need. It's the oxygen mask analogy. Place your mask on yourself first, so that you have what you need to assist others. We want to be an asset, and also we don't want to be a liability. At all times, it is our choice to bring the best of who we are and what we have to offer to the table. This is what making an impact is about. We serve from our place of brilliance with the support of our achievements and in alignment with our purpose and mission.

Zone of Impact is about both what impacts me and how I impact others. We are all meant to be impacted by the impact we have on the world around us.

Knowing WHY you are here — what you are meant to experience, learn and do, and how you are to grow, influence and impact your environments — permits you to better understand where your value is most valuable and also most valued.

It allows you to focus on the supports and conditions under which you perform at your best and are most positively impactful. It holds you accountable to a level of responsibility that comes from you showing up in your value and with your chosen approach. Impact is about more than just who you are and how you are; it's about how both of these aspects, collectively, leave a lasting impression on everything else around you.

How often do you think about the ripple effect of your thoughts, words, choices and actions? How intentional are you about how you want to leave something (a person, place or experience) after you have engaged with it?

I remember one of the earliest impressions that my mother made on me as a child. She always used to tell me to look at where I could leave something better than I found it. Whether it be a person, a place or a situation, she had me constantly thinking about my Zone of Impact.

Now, it is always important not to extract any part of the equation Zone of Brilliance + Zone of Achievement = Zone of Impact and make our focus all about that piece. To leave a positive impact doesn't just mean DOING something to improve, shape or mindfully influence our environment. Sometimes, it's about allowing others to find their own way (not doing it for them) or holding space for a solution to come on its own.

Zone of Impact is always about BOTH how we are BEING and what we choose to DO to support that way of being. It's really more about being congruent and in alignment with ourselves, so that we can fit into this world in the exact way we are meant to fit, making the exact impact we are here to make.

When we are too caught up in trying to be a certain way or doing things that we think are expected of us to make a particular impact, we rarely make the impression we are truly meant to make. This is why it is so important to understand our Zone of Brilliance and Zone of Achievement and where each plays its role so that we can best understand how to show up in our Zone of Impact.

Defining Your Zone of Impact – The Process

- List the words that describe characteristics that positively impact you, as well as how you want to impact others and what you want to leave behind as your legacy. Consider the question, "when others think about me and my work, what adjectives would they use?"

For example, I am very positively motivated and inspired by people and in environments that are focused on intentional growth. I thrive and am impacted in such a way that it keeps me intentional about my own growth and betterment, desiring to impact others by creating opportunities for them to also be intentionally growth oriented.

- Narrow your chosen list down to the top five impact words that reflect your mission and the legacy you want to leave behind.

- You can use your chosen words to complete the following statement: *"At my core, my mission is to facilitate … and this is the impact I wish to make at all times."* Work with these from a point of intention around how you wish to bring them into your day-to-day interactions and engagements.

Discovering and Developing Our Inner Leadership Model: Consideration #3 – Leaving the Legacy That Others Need

"You are far more powerful than you think. Don't abdicate your power. In every interaction, your perspective sets the stage for how the other person responds to you. Your perspective determines the quality of your relationships. If the other person is whiny, your perspective sets the stage for them to be more whiny — or less. If the other person is acting needy, your perspective sets the stage for them to act more needy — or less. If the other person is controlling, your perspective set the stage for them to be more controlling — or less. Your perspective plays a huge role in your outcome and the outcome of others."

This quote comes from one of my favorite parable books, *Yes, You Can Change the World* by Aman Motwane. The book tells the story of a father's legacy and points out the various ways in which we influence and impact others throughout our lives, simply by being who and how we are.

Despite what we have been conditioned to believe, who others need us to be is not about listening to what the outside world tells us about this. It IS about determining, as previously mentioned, who we came to be, and from this place, what we are meant to do and how, as well as what we are here to leave behind. This is not something we can learn from others. It is something we must discover within ourselves. This is not only about authenticity, truth and legacy, it's about what we came here to experience and how we came to grow and develop. Our life is not simply a tool to be used for the benefit of others. We are also meant to receive value from who we are and what we were born to build, create and manifest.

A number of years ago, I designed what has become one of my favorite client exercises. It's called the Authentic Life Blueprint. It allows someone to do two things that I know are necessary for manifesting the life each of us came to live: Dreaming and Defining.

When we were children, we would dream about what we wanted to do and be when we grew up. We would create exciting visions in which anything was possible. As we grew older, for many of us, these visions began to become more limited and "realistic" in nature.

Yet, to dream is to reach into our deepest well of desire and bring to the surface our authentic wants. We have these wants because we are meant to.

How often do you focus on what you truly want?

And why is this?

As I often say to clients, I have come to believe that our greatest gifts (Zone of Brilliance), as well as our unique approach (Zone of Achievement), are not all that we are meant to acknowledge and honor. It is the wants and desires within us that we are also meant to recognize and have. I'm not talking about the surface wants or the dysfunctional ones; I'm referring to the deep, wholehearted and individual wants that each of us holds securely in our hearts. These are the desires we know will help support us in our greatest greatness to fulfill our legacy by showing up fully in our Zone of Impact.

So, ask yourself, "What do I truly want?"

Then allow yourself the answer that comes from deep within. Make a space for it in the foundational considerations and decisions of your day to day.

We are meant to create, act and live these deep wants.

This is so much a part of why we came to this glorious life.

Allowing ourselves to put on paper the way we would like our life to be provides us the opportunity to take a step closer to claiming that life, which IS our legacy in this world. When we do so with an open mind and heart, we permit ourselves to embrace the dream and to continue to take the steps to bring what we see is possible into reality.

When we write, we do so through the use of language. The words we choose define the meaning of what we are envisioning. Therefore, as previously stated, choosing our words intentionally is essential. Paying special attention to the language we use when communicating our dreams on paper (in our heads or out loud) is crucial.

How we say something leads to how we continue to identify and understand it. This influences our feelings, actions and the responses we have to it. When that "it" is the vision we have of our very own life, we can see how paramount it is that we take the time to consider, shape and select our words wisely and from a place of real possibility. Otherwise, we may risk creating something we don't want. If we don't consider what we want at all, we can end up leaving our life up to chance and to the charge of our inner default mechanisms (conditioning, limiting beliefs, fears, etc.).

Oftentimes, the challenge to defining what we want is warming up to the practice of dreaming.

"I'm not really sure what I want," many people say to me. This is fair, because quite a few of us have not really allowed ourselves the luxury of considering what it is we really, truly want from the place of knowing we can have it, or from the place of understanding its role when it comes to creating the legacy that others also need from us.

The world needs us to live our biggest, brightest and most brilliant life. We have all been given the potential to make our very best impact, and we do this most effectively when we allow ourselves to dig deep and define what we see.

In Act 2, you have had the opportunity to create your inner leadership model by seeking engagement with and defining your 3 Zones. In Act 3, you'll learn how and why it's crucial to accept ownership of and have agency over your unique leadership lane. We'll discuss how to align, integrate and implement your 3 Zones to create a sense of sovereignty and control over your life and how you live it.

ACT 3

Accepting Ownership:
Aligning, Integrating and
Implementing the 3 Zones

"Being able to speak and live with the truth, your truth, means you have to become comfortable with having your power, be comfortable with all that is true about you and all that is beautiful within yourself. This is being okay with who and what you are."

—Caroline Myss

THIS QUOTE ALWAYS MAKES ME THINK OF ANOTHER ONE BY MARIANNE WILLIAMSON FROM HER BOOK *A RETURN TO LOVE*.

"Our deepest fear is not that we are inadequate. Our deepest fear is that we are powerful beyond measure. It is our light, not our darkness that most frightens us. We ask ourselves, who am I to be brilliant, gorgeous, talented, fabulous? Actually, who are you not to be?

Your playing small does not serve the world. There is nothing enlightened about shrinking so that other people won't feel insecure around you. We are all meant to shine, as children do. We were born to manifest the glory within us. It is not just in some of us; it is in everyone. And as we let our own light shine, we unconsciously give other people permission to do the same. As we are liberated from our own fear, our presence automatically liberates others."

Accepting the truth of who we are and how we want to live, create and impact the world can be a real process. It's one thing to become aware of what we have to give and how we would like to deliver this value. It's quite another to completely embrace and own this knowledge, which is to embody these truths and fully identify with them.

In my work with clients over the years, I have witnessed a funny thing that people do. In fact, I refer to it as the Greatest Irony. It's this: The things that are most valuable about us, we either don't see at all as a value or we actually consider them imperfections, sometimes even detriments.

An example is my client, Phillip. (name has been changed for confidentiality) He's a real genius. I'm talking a visionary of the likes of Steve Jobs and Elon Musk. As you can imagine, Phillip is light-years ahead of most people in his ability to envision the future and to understand how things connect on a larger scale. He is also tremendously evolved in the way in which he thinks, processes and communicates.

The first conversation I had with Phillip was about his concern over being misunderstood, as well as coming across as "cocky" or arrogant when interacting with others, because of the level at which he comprehends things and expresses himself. Phillip is also a very people-oriented guy, and he sees his life 100 percent as one of service. In my interactions with him, he always struck me as an extremely humble, sometimes even self-deprecating person.

In our first discussion, I asked Phillip, "What if you could be completely assured there was no chance of ever being arrogant in any of your interactions and engagements with others?"

His response was, "That would be great! Where do I sign up?"

I chuckled and told him, "It only takes seeing your true value, understanding your purpose and mission and setting the intention of how you want to impact others in your interactions and engagements."

Phillip looked at me intently, and I continued.

"The person you are is one of innate humility and focus on other. With this kind of DNA, you can be more concerned that you will magically transform into a gorilla than be arrogant. It's simply not in your makeup. Now, that's not to say others might not translate your actions as arrogant. This is very different from BEING arrogant. We cannot control the meaning and story others give to who we are and what we are doing, but we can control the story WE tell ourselves about who and how we are. Each of us has 100 percent command over how we see ourselves and acknowledging and being who we want to be and acting in alignment with this."

"So, what I hear you saying is I only need to concern myself with seeing who I am and being who I am?" Phillip said to me, slowly. "My job is to understand what that is and commit to aligning with my authentic nature through my intentional thoughts, feelings and actions?"

"Exactly," I responded with a grin. "You now get to begin the journey of owning who you are."

My dear friend, Helen Moses, is a speech and communications coach. In her book, *Voice Unleashed*, she wrote, "Just as standing in good posture increases the impact of our voices, living in alignment unleashes our potential. It frees us from the prisons of fear, shame, embarrassment and worry. When we turn on our light and stand in it, the world is bright with possibilities, joy and love. Our priorities become clear. Being in alignment with your unique gifts and passions opens doors for opportunities you may never have even been able to dream before."

Of course, there are certainly things about us that for obvious reasons we may be challenged to own. What occurs when we see traits and characteristics within ourselves that are far less shiny than our greatest gifts? After all, we are not only the beautiful and powerful qualities within us, we are the shadowy and challenged parts, too. Owning who and what we are means accepting and integrating all aspects of ourselves, and this starts with looking at them and being honest about what we see and what we wish to do about it.

We all are quite familiar with the fairy tale *Snow White*. In the story, Snow White's evil step-mother relies upon her magic mirror to affirm her superiority in all things great, powerful and beautiful.

How often do we, too, turn to the outside world to be our mirror and show us things about ourselves that we deeply want and need to believe are true?

We may surround ourselves with others, put ourselves in situations and make choices that will portray us in our best light and make it comfortable and possible for us to feel good about ourselves and safe in the world.

Now what happens, like in *Snow White*, when what that mirror shows us is something we don't want to see or are resistant to believing? What do we do then?

The answer to this can be a starting point from which we can begin to unravel and clearly see the places where we hold ourselves back from being at our best and greatest.

As a coach, I have worked to support others in answering this question for themselves and to glean and capitalize on what is illuminated for the purpose of betterment.

I have also worked very hard, myself, toward self-improvement. Over the years, I have had the chance to dig into this particular question on plenty of occasions.

Each time, it has provided me the opportunity to uncover beliefs, patterns and points at which I have allowed myself to go "off road" and turn away from the me I want to be, the true person I am.

My own mirror has given me powerful reflections of where I have been undervaluing myself and others (both people and situations) and how by doing this time and again in my life, I have created an environment and way of being where I haven't had to show up fully and most brilliantly.

I want to point out something very important here: These findings and realizations are not something for which I am choosing to feel shame or bad about myself. They are, quite clearly for me, an opportunity to change. When these situations occur, they provide a tremendous chance to get to the root of what I have done, believed and followed that has kept me from knowing and owning myself. They have provided the opportunity to become aware of where I have been staying smaller and less engaged in my life and in the true service I came here to perform.

When speaking about and looking at the importance of accepting and seeing the value of all aspects of who I am when it comes to owning myself and my potential, it is true that the lesser parts of me allow the shinier ones to be seen even more fully. We see this in drawings when an artist uses the technique of shadow in an area on a sketch, drawing or painting to bring out and highlight the lighter aspects of the image and create a more intense 3D or lifelike effect. It presents an image in its totality.

It is also true that sometimes I have to step away from a merit or standard to know it's there and understand how much I value it. Each of my own moments of acknowledgment, around aspects of myself and/or my behavior that do not represent the person or purpose I'm here to uphold, has permitted me to arrive at a place of acceptance and understanding. Each has allowed me to recognize things about myself that I have not wanted to acknowledge, admit or own. This has made me more resilient, cognizant, intentional, humble, wise and simply better.

By observing what I'm not wanting to be, I have been able to better define who I am. By witnessing myself with more clarity, I can view others as they truly are, as well.

I have also learned what I am uncomfortably willing to do for myself and others to make room for necessary change and growth. To step away from what is known to be whole, healthy and authentic. To be able to move forward into the light and not hide in the shadows of half-truths and limiting beliefs and behaviors. To be able to look, squarely, at a version of myself who is not who I came here to be and to find excitement in what I can embrace instead.

I feel these new depths that I've been reaching, by looking honestly and without reservation and resistance into my MIRROR ON THE WALL, have allowed me to wake up to new recognitions of truth and possibility.

How amazing is it that the lessons we repeat over and over can bring us to a new launching point and awareness that the many years of training have delivered us here, in this moment, to purposefully create the intentional life that we have always wanted for ourselves.

It's like an Olympic athlete who has trained his/her whole life for a single event. In a singular moment of choice, looking back on all that has been learned and accomplished, NOW is the time to apply the experiences and to do so fully engaged, awake and conscious, putting everything on the line and being in it to win it!

What I have learned about this aspect of owning ourselves is this: To effectively use our mirror and understand that the world out there is a mere reflection of our inner world, first we must be comfortable and ready to receive whatever it is that is reflected back to us. We must know that it's not ultimately about what it shows us. What we choose to do with what we see makes all the difference.

Of course, all of this takes patience and a willingness to work and get comfortable in the unknown. Finding and owning ourselves can often feel like walking through an unfamiliar forest in the dark. We stumble and feel around for what we seek, much of the time not even knowing if we are going in the right direction.

The Power of Leading from Our Lane with Intention

When I first created my WHAT-HOW-WHERE model, the one that eventually led me to develop the 3 Zones, I decided to test its functionality and viability in my own life. I went through the process of defining my Innate Value, my desired Approach to delivering this value and my ideal Environments/Experiences that most effectively supported me to perform and show up at my best.

With my list of five words for each, I applied these definitions to every interaction and experience that I had.

Before jumping out of bed in the morning, I quietly and intentionally thought about my value, approach and the outcomes or environment I wanted to create in my interactions with my husband and daughter. A few moments before every client call, I ran through what I felt my value, approach and environmental influence was when it came to my role as coach. Before entering any meeting, get-together or engagement, I contemplated my words to remind me of what I had to offer, how I wanted to offer it and what environmental outcomes I wished to create.

To say the least, this first year of guinea pigging my new model had me living an uber intentional life. In the beginning, it took a lot of time and discipline to reroute behaviors and create these new patterns, but after a while, it started to simply become how I did things.

I could have never known how much this new practice had to teach me, until about six months into it, I was invited to speak at a national women's event. I was asked to present on the importance of self-care and simple ways to incorporate self-supporting practices into these women's busy day-to-day lives.

As I prepared to enter the building where I would deliver my presentation to 200+ women, I took a moment to close my eyes, breathe and run through my words. I reminded myself of what I was there to be and do. I considered the role and the material I was hired to deliver and the value I was to offer. I thought about how I wanted this to look, feel and be. I envisioned the delivery of the material and how the women would receive it. I took the time to feel how this would support my audience to practice better self-care. Finally, I visualized where this experience would take me and my audience. I contemplated what we all would gain from being together and learning and sharing.

It's worth mentioning that my words for that day were as follows:

What: *Truthful, Relevant, Thoughtful, Intentional and Observant*

How: *Supportive, Kind, Initiating, Respectful and Confident*

Where: *Real, Connective, Illuminating, Healing and Transformational*

The room was large, with about 10 women seated at each of the 20 round tables filling the space. Event staff and others lined the back of the room. It was a full house.

About halfway into my talk, I was in the midst of presenting information on the importance of how we nourish ourselves through food choice, when one of the women in the audience stood up and began yelling at me. Apparently, she had taken offense to something I had quoted from the doctor whose research I was sharing that discussed the relationship between nutrition and mental health.

The woman called me names, pointed, swore and demanded that I be asked to leave for presenting such insulting material. Everyone in the room was stunned. The MC attempted to step in to regain some control over what was going on, but I found myself holding up my hand and asking to allow the woman her time. Everyone looked at me, questioningly.

Finally, the woman, with the help of her friends seated around her, settled down and sat in her seat. She calmed down enough to shift from yelling to speaking loudly, and then finally she stopped altogether.

Again, the MC stepped up to take the mic, and I asked if I could address what had just transpired. She nodded, I believe, not really knowing what to do, but looking somewhat relieved that it seemed someone did.

The room was silent. I began, looking straight at the woman slumped in her seat. "First, I would like to thank you for sharing what I can imagine was very uncomfortable for you. It's clear that something I said was deeply triggering for you, and I want you to know that my intention was never to come here to cause distress or anger." I stopped. In that moment, it hit me, and I continued. "In fact, I can tell you exactly what my intentions were."

At that point, I shared with all of the women my work with the WHAT-HOW-WHERE words that had become my intentional beacon for six months. I told them the words I had practiced and reminded myself of just before arriving to give my presentation. I expressed to them that it seemed having these words did, in fact, have a powerful ability to direct the outcome of things.

I watched the faces of the women in that room. I looked into the eyes of the woman who had just, 10 minutes before, been yelling at me. Tears were streaming down her face. She was nodding her head, and she looked very sad and extremely guilt-ridden.

I spoke to her again. "Without intention, we are all walking around, potentially ready to react to whatever comes our way. When we go through life on autopilot, we create accidental lives. When we are intentional about our whats, hows, wheres and whys, we can finally experience a more conscious and deliberate existence."

The woman stared back at me, unmoving. I could see her breath rise and fall within her chest. She was taking in my words. She was considering what she thought and how she felt. It was good. The room remained silent, and I spoke again.

"I have to be honest, I'm quite surprised that I'm standing here in front of all of you addressing all of this the way I am. I'm no more noble and proficient at being calm, centered and grounded during times of uncertainty than anyone else, but what I feel I do have right now is intention. Let me share with you what happened to me when all of this first began. When I first heard the yelling and what was being said, I found myself going in and straight to the WHAT-HOW-WHERE words that I shared with you. Like going over a checklist, I began to consider each of my words, asking myself if I thought I had been, had done or was creating what that word represented. With each check, I could see that I was good. I was congruent with what I set out to do and be. When I got to the end of my words, I realized that none of what was occurring was about me. It was about something else, and because I had nothing to be defensive about or try to control, I realized, in a moment, that I could be open and available to continue to do, be and create in alignment with my intentions. I recognized that I was in the position to deliver something that was completely off script, but that was needed more than what was in my presentation notes."

That is when I was stunned for the second time that day. One at a time, each of the women seated in the room began to stand up and applaud. After a few minutes, I was receiving a standing ovation.

After my talk, I was gathering up my things and preparing to leave, when the woman who had taken issue with some of my material approached me. She took my hands.

"I want to thank you," she said, simply. "I've always been like this, you know. Reactive and prone to confrontation. No one, however, has ever responded to my direct attacks the way you did today: with love, generosity and understanding. You taught us all so much about how to be a really good human. I want you to know I'm going home, and I'm finally going to seek help. I don't want to be a defensive powder keg ready to blow. I want to be more intentional."

As I watched her walk away, I thought, again, of

the influence and outcome words I had chosen for my presentation: Real, Connective, Illuminating, Healing and Transformational. Check, check, check, check and CHECK.

Implementing the 3 Zones:

The act of intentionally applying your zone definitions to your daily life IS the implementation process. (Refer back to Act 2 for the steps on how to define your zones.)

So, let's take a moment to review the 3 Zones.

Zone 1: Who We Are Here to Be —
Our Zone of Brilliance

Zone 2: How We Are Here to Be —
Our Zone of Achievement

Zone 3: Why We Are Here (mission and purpose) —
Our Zone of Impact

Zone of Brilliance + Zone of Achievement
= Zone of Impact

Applying the definitions you have selected for each of your zones to your day-to-day interactions and engagements allows for more flow and alignment within you and your experiences. It also creates more intentional impact and outcomes in your life.

The Role of Control

To fully understand and appreciate the importance of taking the time to develop and implement our 3 Zones, we must first look at what challenges us to do this, consistently or at all.

Here, I'd like to take some time to discuss the influence human conditions and social/cultural trends can have on our ability to fully own, integrate and implement our Zones.

In his book *Willpower Doesn't Work,* author Benjamin Hardy makes this bold statement:

"The environment around us is far too powerful, stimulating, addicting and stressful to overcome by white knuckling. The only way to stop just surviving and learn to truly thrive in today's world is to create and control your environment."

Hardy goes on to add that "controlling" our environment is NOT about exerting our WILL in order to do so. Instead, it's about choosing and influencing our external environment through getting right internally in our mindset, behaviors and approach. In other words, controlling ourselves, in regard to who we are, and how we respond and choose through our thoughts, actions and environments.

Proof that willpower doesn't work is where many people find themselves when they encounter unexpected change and react by trying to control it. If you attempt to manage an unknown situation the way you might take on a diet or exercise regimen geared toward losing weight because you don't like the way you look or your doctor told you it's a requirement, you'll know what I'm talking about. Applying willpower to "force" ourselves into new behaviors does not create sustainable change. When change is required, we are, ultimately, being asked to transform in some way. If we simply try to control things based on what we fear or what we think will make us feel safe and comfortable, this practice will leave us feeling depleted and frustrated.

When we become fatigued by a situation or process, what we may be experiencing is exactly what we'd see before falling off that diet or exercise regime or any band-aid fix we have chosen to address the REAL, INTERNAL shift we want to feel and experience. It's an exhaustion that comes from running out of fuel and "push."

If we have been "waiting it out" and simply managing our situations, hoping for issues to "go away" or improve from our efforts to control them, we may want to consider things differently. What we are most likely experiencing is not about the band-aid pivot just to attempt to control the environmental factors we are experiencing. It's about finding ways to truly and deeply integrate the shifts and changes necessary to make the new behaviors into a lifestyle and not a "diet" to help us survive a temporary blip or overcome a short-term obstacle.

There are many things I don't know, but one thing I do know is we can never "go back" to the way things were. There is only forward, and the future is meant to look and feel different. That's what growth is about: moving forward and being challenged to constantly find ways to create alignment with who we are, how we are and why we are here.

What all of this asks of us is to take more personal responsibility for the choices and actions we take that create the experiences and circumstances in our lives. As a collective, we are constantly commanded to work on ways to both support and challenge one another TO BE more responsible and accountable.

One of my favorite models for awareness and personal accountability discusses the dynamics we tend to engage in when we are under stress.

In the late 1960s, psychiatrist Dr. Stephen Karpman created the Drama Triangle roles and discussed their interplay as a model to demonstrate the most common ways in which people interact (through ego) in an attempt to govern their fears and anxiety.

Later, showing how to consciously move beyond these drama roles, author David Emerald created the TED model to illustrate how humans can shift from states/roles of disempowerment to take positive control of their lives. In his book *The Power of TED*, through the use of parable, Emerald lays out how to gain awareness of the roles we are playing and how to choose and act from more empowering positions where necessary.

The key to the triangle models is understanding what constitutes each disempowerment role, how the roles play off of one another and what strategies can be used to shift into the positions and perspectives that allow us to act from a place of effectiveness and empowerment within our own mindsets and in our interactions with others.

To see lasting external improvement, we get to learn what produces temporary, and often ineffective, fixes. Taking the time to see where the meaning we ascribe to things manifests into the reality we experience is crucial. Understanding where we play roles in generating what we experience is a necessary part of cultivating the empowerment we covet.

We only have the ability to effectively implement our 3 Zones and create healthy boundaries in our lives when we comprehend and are conscious of these situational dynamics and our role(s) in them. Simply pushing for change isn't enough. We must BE the change we desire.

Taking control of the stories you tell and the roles you play within them to design the life you want takes awareness, dedication, practice and resiliency. Using the triangle models as a powerful tool can help you to become more focused on what you CAN do to shift what and how you create and experience things. Being more conscious, intentional and responsible in your life will support your ability to actively and successfully implement your 3 Zones and create the sense of empowerment and fulfillment that you seek in all of your various interactions and engagements.

So, let's take a look at how the "role of control" might look in leadership. Here, a conversation I had with one of my clients presents an opportunity to view how we can create better outcomes. When focused on our power to lead through our 3 Zones, we can invite others into empowerment, instead of attempting to exert control over people and situations.

"I feel like I'm losing control," my client blurted out at the start of our session. "I simply don't seem to have any power over my employees."

I sat for a moment and then responded. "What would it look like for you to be in power within your business?"

He reflected for a bit, then said, "I guess my employees would be following directions and doing what I ask of them. I would not feel like I have to constantly babysit everyone to ensure they were doing what I hired them to do."

"And I'm guessing this current situation that you are describing is pretty exhausting for you," I said.

"You got that right!" my client exclaimed. "I can't focus on what I need to do to grow the company because I'm always having to double-check everyone's work, handle dropped balls with clients and have what seems like endless conversations about expectations and where they aren't being met."

I paused and said, "It sounds to me like you've given your power away by choosing to approach the situation from a position of disempowerment. Because of this, you are creating an environment where to feel in control, you expect your employees to also give up their power. No wonder you are experiencing things as out of control. No one seems to be empowered, and that's why you see the behaviors you are witnessing."

"Oh boy," was all my client said.

I went on. "What if you found a way where everyone can be empowered, and you can achieve the outcomes you desire?"

"That's what I want. It's no fun to be the one always feeling like I have to make everything happen," my client replied with an exasperated sigh.

"I can imagine it isn't," I said. "The important thing to do now is to understand how and where the power relinquishment and control expectation happen and determine what gets to change."

My client remained silent. I continued.

"When we think in terms of being in power, we often unconsciously follow a course of action that positions us to have our power taken from us, or more aptly put, to be disempowered. In actuality, the only true power we have is in our choice. After we make that choice, everything that comes from it is out of our control. You want your choice to have influence in its power to create a desired outcome."

My client laughed softly. "Is that why you recently suggested I read the book *Power vs Force* by David Hawkins? I started it, and in the preface, he wrote something that I'm seeing applies to what you are saying. I actually wrote it right here in my coaching journal. 'We think we live by forces we control, but in fact, we are governed by power from unrevealed sources, power over which we have no control.' When I read that, I knew it was something I would need to remember."

I laughed. "That's wonderful! You are beginning to recognize the dots and connect them. This is a very significant first step! So, we are looking at a situation where you have felt you needed to control your employees for them to do what you need them to do. Is that a fair assessment?"

"I would say it is, yes," my client replied.

"Okay," I said, "and now you see that this sense of control that you strive for is not something you can actually attain. When you attempt to enforce power over others, you create situations where you feel more and more out of control, because you are meant to experience exactly that — the fact you are, indeed, not in control. The control you think you seek is an illusion, and your choice to seek it has you operating in a disempowered state."

"Hmmm, yes, so what do I do instead?" my client asked.

"Well, I'd say that you want to look for approaches that shift the focus of having power over your employees to creating opportunities for them to harness and utilize their own power in healthy, fulfilling and productive ways. Invite everyone to engage in dynamics that are empowering. Right now, it sounds like your people are engaging in unhealthy ways in reaction to your attempts to control them. With this new awareness, you now have the chance to develop empowerment situations, both for yourself and your employees."

"Wow, yeah, I can totally see this," my client enthusiastically responded. "How do I do that?"

My reply was simple. "By understanding the true impact Control, Power and Empowerment have in your engagements. Are you in front of your computer?"

"I am."

"Great! Google the definition of control and read it to me."

"Got it," he replied. "It says, 'the power to influence or direct people's behavior or course of events.'"

"Okay," I replied. "Now, look up the definition for power."

"Power — the capacity or ability to direct or influence the behavior of others or the course of events. Wow, that's the same definition!"

"It is," I said, "and is it true based on what we have discussed? Can you truly direct or influence the behavior of others or the course of events?"

"Not unless they choose to allow me to or give their power away to me," my client said slowly.

"That's right," I replied, equally slowly. "And is this what you want? For your employees to give their power over to you, so that you can control their behavior to ensure that things go exactly as you would like?"

"No, not at all!" my client responded emphatically. "I would like my team to want to do their jobs and help create an environment of support and a culture of collaboration and community."

"Alright," I said, "so this is what you need to do. Create an environment of support and a culture of collaboration and community. What this would take is for everyone to be empowered to direct all operations and engagement toward a commonly held and acknowledged goal. Do you agree?"

"That's right, yes, I do," my client replied.

"Okay, now let's have you look up the definition of empower and empowerment," I said.

"Empower — to give the authority or power to someone to do something.

Empowerment — The process of becoming stronger and more confident, especially in controlling one's own life and claiming one's rights."

"Which approach do you feel will render the results you're going for?" I asked.

My client chuckled. "Well, I believe that's pretty obvious, considering the fact that I now know the way I have been going about things will never work or provide the experience and outcomes I want — for myself or my team."

"Outstanding awareness," I said. "I'd also like to offer, perhaps, an even better definition for empower based on today's conversation and for you to consider moving forward:

Empower — to allow and offer opportunities for the power of others to be recognized, honored and utilized in healthy, fulfilling and productive ways."

"Oh, I like that," said my client. "I'm writing that down now!"

I smiled. "It asks of you to think in terms of how you set up your communications, operations, protocol and engagements to be in alignment with this definition. Creating community is different from creating a ruler-ship. As we look at this through the lens of what we have discussed, it's not about giving someone else the author-ity or power to do something, when what we are really looking at is the sovereign power of another. We simply do not have this control, and we need to see this if we want to establish a culture of buy-in, ownership and ulti-mate sustainable growth where everyone has and knows their value and their rightful zone of genius. It's not force or control that can provide this — it's empowerment."

"I can truly see that now," my client said earnestly. "More importantly, I can feel it. I look forward to discussing and developing ways to shift the control paradigm in my own approach to things. I want to show up better and reserve my energy for where it can be best utilized and where it provides the highest contribution."

Giving Our Power Away: The Trends of Safetyism and Fragility

In the book *The Coddling of the American Mind,* authors Greg Lukianoff and Jonathan Haidt present stories and data around current trends that reflect a culture less capable of handling challenge, and therefore, less able to grow and build resiliency. In a word, we are becoming increasingly fragile.

Since the beginning of 2020, we have certainly seen how this time has put a spotlight on American fragility when it comes to our health, finances, governmental systems, education, overall mindset and how we have learned to get along.

Since the early 2000s, there has been growing interest and focus on social change and the inequities within our culture. This has bred a desire for swifter justice, truth and new ways of defining what is "right" and what is "safe." It has also paved the way for heightened polarization and the escalation of an ever-growing Us vs. Them call-out culture.

For this reason, knowing who we are, how we are and why we are here is becoming increasingly crucial. In the world in which we live, it is far too easy to get swept up in the cultural pressures that are being placed on us around what to believe, how to act and who to be. Our security, safety and sense of belonging are critically tied to the choices we make around each of these things.

In Lukianoff's and Haidt's conversation about safetyism, we see situations and triggers as unsafe and dangerous, that in previous times were considered and labeled as uncomfortable aspects of life. This has created a highly reactive culture that is developing a greater weakness for navigating challenges and growth. Emerging beliefs that the culture, environments and those in charge are responsible for making things safe and comfortable physically and emotionally for all individuals is creating a loss of individual responsiblity, accountability and personal agency.

With the rise of safetyism, there has been a loss of resilience and autonomy in our culture and an increase in victim mentality, fear-based thinking and fragility. The belief that it isn't up to oneself to develop measures to handle and navigate life's challenges, but that it is the obligation of the external environment to make things safe and comfortable has weakened many individuals' ability to cope and see themselves as confident and capable.

When we don't feel capable of creating something for ourselves, we turn to others to do this for us. When we don't know who we are, how we are meant to show up and why we are here, we will be less self-directed, self-confident and self-sufficient. We will be more inclined to believe we need to rely on what is outside of us to create the surety and guidance that we are unable to access internally. We will be at the mercy of what this outside world creates for us and does "to" us, because we will not see that by looking out instead of building within, we are relinquishing our soveign right to determine, create and live our own, authentic lives.

The trends of safetyism and fragility have also affected many of the rights that we have as humans. Within the United States, changing norms around beliefs regarding the freedom of speech and what is considered safe and dangerous have intensified tendencies to evaluate the content of speech more offensively, making it less about the right to speak and more about who gets to speak and what gets to be said. Demands that free speech rights be taken away from those who are perceived to be causing emotional or physical harm through what they say are much more common across all social groups.

Something to consider is that when we dictate who can speak and what is allowable, we no longer have freedom of speech. It also takes away our free will to choose what we will do with the information someone is sharing. Each of us has choice when it comes to what we do with what others say. When others have the right to say what they want, we get to practice our own right to take responsibility for our will and choice, and not blame the words of others for the thoughts, stories, beliefs and actions that we choose to create from those words. When we take the right to speak freely away from individuals, we also take away our right to take responsibility for our responses and for how we choose to control ourselves, because this is effectively being done for us.

To overcome and disengage from practices that build safetyism and fragility, we must cultivate our own free agency and accept that discomfort is a necessary ingredient for growth, responsibility, accountability and self-sovereignty. Yes, we get to speak up for injustice and what we want to see change in this world, but doing it through taking rights from others or expecting that we will always be safe and situations will be controlled while doing so will not get us what we ultimately want and need. The art of debate and being introduced to various perspectives and viewpoints is necessary to build a true, diverse, inclusive, and innovating culture.

The longer we resist and continue to focus on the "oh how awfuls," the "blame/shame game," "us vs. them" thinking and being a culture that cannot be uncomfortable, the longer it will take for us to grow in a positive direction, and the more discomfort we will experience. After all, what we resist, persists.

As has always been the case, we all need to be willing to go through what is necessary to level up and move things to a higher and greater place. Each and every one of us is responsible to do this for and within ourselves, and we begin by learning and practicing how to align, integrate and implement our 3 Zones.

Eight years ago, I had a hit of divine inspiration while driving. This download came in the form of a book title, *The Conscious CEO.* At the time, the idea of conscious leadership hadn't yet emerged, but I could feel it was on the fringes. As I considered what this book would be about, my mind went to top industry leaders. These were the executives at the helm of some of the largest corporations in the world.

The thought was this: What if these leaders were able to have deeply transformational "coming home" experiences where they became clear about who they were and what true and positive impact they were here to make? What would this mean for their own life experience and sense of fulfillment? How would this impact both those around them and those whose lives their industries touched?

Two weeks later, I was offered the opportunity to work with leaders who had been incarcerated in federal prison. My three-year stint helping facilitate a men's transformational program taught me more than I could ever have learned elsewhere about what it truly looked and felt like at the top. The high stakes, expectations and loneliness. It became my mission to work with top leaders to help them transform into the men and women they came to be and lead from this sovereign and authentic place.

Fast-forward to today. Much has already begun to emerge in this arena of conscious leadership. The year 2020 challenged us in many ways. It also permitted us to slow down and take stock. Going into our homes during the quarantine provided the opportunity for many to come home to themselves and discover, define and align more of what their hearts and creative centers had been calling them to acknowledge and reconcile.

At the time this book is published, the current leadership model is beckoning us to develop higher levels of emotional and instinctive intelligence. Our desire to understand and connect with people is leading the charge, and human-based leadership models are rolling out faster than the Model T coming off the first mass production assembly line in 1913.

This time feels and is chaotic because everything is changing. In the years to come, we are going to see massive innovation in what we can do and offer and in how we communicate these offerings. We will also be expected to increase our leadership quotient, as we are called to begin to build the procedures and systems needed to support a new paradigm.

Heart and intuitive leadership will lead us all into the development of more diverse, agile, collaborative and inclusionary practices and cultures. It will force us to think even more intentionally and build from our individual and collective core values and visionary goals.

We cannot simply give lip service to these new ideas, approaches and practices either. It can and will be rightfully challenging to lead others who have opinions and perspectives that are different and, in some cases, counter-intuitive to the way we want to lead and govern.

We must be, legitimately, concerned and curious about the interests and needs of others and how our decisions impact them. We must refine our capacity to listen and learn, to be humbled regularly and to turn from the need to look good and be right, comfortable and safe in order to feel "in charge."

We must learn to respect and make room for thoughts, perspectives and ways of doing things that are different from our own without creating cultures of polarity and separatism. It will take commitment, reflection, a willingness to fail and try again, and lots and lots of humility.

The good news is that when we are truly coming from a place of collective-centeredness, this work becomes far easier. At our core, we all want connection, and all of these things breed connection.

Paul Keijzer, a leader in helping transform top teams and manage talent across emerging markets, says, "I am of the firm belief that the first and foremost hallmark of a good leader is their ability to make their employees feel special. These leaders are generous when it comes to giving due recognition to the contributions that each team member brings to the company because they take the time to get to know their employees on a personal front. Remember that your style of leadership depends on the conscious and subconscious rules you apply to the workplace. What you give to your team and how you practice decision-making are critical aspects of leadership."

So, as you use the models and suggestions from this book to continue developing yourself as a leader, I invite you to use a heart and intuitive-centered lens as you give meaning and apply action to the various experiences that you have. As you open yourself up to practicing what

has been discussed here, there will be plenty of chances
to listen to what your inner voice is saying and where it
wants to lead you.

I recommend you listen and allow yourself to be
transformed by the process.

CURTAIN CALL
Leadership Development:
The Importance of Wading

"At its best, leadership development is not an 'event,' it's a capacity-building endeavor. It's a process of human growth and maturation."

—Linda Fisher Thornton

As Peter F. Drucker once said, "Leadership is an achievement of trust," and as John C. Maxwell says, "Leadership development is a lifetime journey, not a quick trip." Both of these quotations make me think of a conversation I had with a long-time friend a number of years ago.

"It's been like wading in the water," my friend had said to me.

"More than just dipping your feet in, but not completely immersed, swimming or diving in either. Just wading . . . hanging out, taking in the newness of the experience, letting it sink in . . . not really understanding the full significance of being in the water, but trusting there is one."

I had smiled. Great analogy, I thought.

He was talking about the work he has been doing to better understand his own value, passions and purpose in this life, not only as a leader, but as a human. He was sharing what he had learned about the process of absorbing the new perspectives, lessons and considerations that had been placed before him.

"I'm understanding the importance of showing up,"

he said. "I don't have to figure out all the hows and whys. I get to be there and bring what I have to give and my intention to help others with me. What I'm seeing is the rest will simply happen."

I had thought, for a moment, about the impact of this statement.

At that time, I had recently had the honor of witnessing the power of what he was describing in his life. What he had become aware of was the result of his ability to allow himself to wade around and be there in all that he had been experiencing.

Letting the waters of change and its life lessons wash over him. Aware, awake, watching without full understanding of what it all truly meant, but with faith that it would lead him to where he needed to be.

It's so interesting when we really look at this point.

We've been conditioned to think in terms of destination. What is our goal? Where do we want to get to next? How do we get from here to there? The focus usually being myopically trained on the "here" and the "there." And then the impatience with the time that it takes for the arrival to happen.

What of the process of getting from one place to another? What is the value of the "hang time" where we are leaping through the air between rocks?

Are the experiences that make up our lives more about where we get to, or are they about the journey we undergo to get there?

Then, what of the knowing?

We are compelled to know, to figure out the hows and the whys. To plot it all out on graphs and charts. To follow directions to a "t" so that we can ensure our outcome.

What is the value of wading here?

Of not exactly knowing . . . yet. Of being present to the experience for the sake of experiencing it. Of learning from the process we are undergoing . . . letting it instruct us instead of us leading it.

Many teach the importance of learning the art of "letting go." The joys of living in the moment and caring more about the minute-to-minute happenings than about how it's all going to work out.

So, if there exist the destination points of life and these are the markers by which we can gauge where we've been and where we would like to go, then the time in between these markers is the "becoming" or unfolding. This process provides the lessons we are to learn that, ultimately, help to guide and support us in life.

I thought about my friend's comment about "showing up," and asked him for a takeaway from this.

"Allowing myself to keep wading," he responded. "Being consistent, open and trusting that I'll eventually get what I'm meant to get."

I nodded.

The value of repetition and consistency is that in the "showing up," time and time again and repeating the same practices over and over, we eventually learn what it all means for us. Knowing that "progress is a process," as another good friend likes to say, is about accepting that the development of anything, whether it's learning how to play golf or how to become a great leader, is also about being unzipped, putting ourselves out there consistently and repeatedly and having faith that you may not "get it" right away, but in time you eventually will.

In this moment of reflection, I thank my friend for his truly awesome way of viewing how to look at the process of learning, growing and being a curious leader. Because of it, I will never again look the same way at the simple act of wading in the waters of life.

Here's to allowing yourself the gift of wading . . .

References

Setting the Stage

Coelho, Paulo, 1988, *The Alchemist*, Harper Collins.

Jensen, Karen, 2016, *Three Brains*, Mind Publishing Inc.

Nischwitz, Jeff, 2014, *Unmask*, Motivational Press Inc.

Hendricks, Gay, 2009, *The Big Leap*, Harper Collins.

Interlude

Greitens, Eric, 2015, *Resilience*, Houghton Mifflin Harcourt Publishing.

Snow, Shane, 2020, "The 4 Most Important (and Rare) Leadership Skills We Need for Our Future," *Forbes* magazine.

Act 1

Clance, P. R., and Imes, S. A., 1978, "The imposter phenomenon in high achieving women: Dynamics and therapeutic intervention," *Psychotherapy: Theory, Research & Practice.*

Abrams, Abigail, 2018, "Yes, Impostor Syndrome is Real. Here's how to Deal with It," *Time* magazine.

"Imposter Syndrome," Zencare, 2020, blog.zencare.co/imposter-syndrome.

Hendricks, Gay, 2009, *The Big Leap*, Harper Collins.

Steves, Rick, 2009, "Circling In On Paris' Arc de Triomphe," *Smithsonian* magazine.

"Facts and Statistics,"Anxiety & Depression Association of America, 2020, adaa.org.

Wickman, Gino, 2016, *Rocket Fuel*, BenBella Books.

Act 2

Griffin, Catherine, 2013, "Why Women Talk More Than Men: Language Protein Uncovered," Science World Report.

Hamann, Lori, 2018, "Keep Your Word (when you have to + how to deal when you don't)," lorihamann.com.

Ward, Paul, 2007, "Sir Ernest Shackleton Endurance Expedition Trans-Antarctica 1914-1917," Cool Antarctica.

Motwane, Aman, 2007, *Yes, You Can Change the World*, Prakash Press.

Act 3

Williamson, Marianne, 1992, *A Return to Love*, Harper Collins.

Moses, Helen, 2020, *Voice Unleashed*, Speak Up Communications.

Hardy, Benjamin, 2018, *Willpower Doesn't Work*, Hachette Books.

"Karpman Drama Triangle." Wikipedia, Wikimedia Foundation, 10 June 2021, en.wikipedia.org/wiki/Karpman_drama_triangle.

Emerald, David, 2016, *The Power of TED*, Polaris Publishing.

Hawkins, David, 1994, *Power vs Force*, Hay House Inc.

Lukianoff, Greg and Haidt, Jonathan, 2018, *The Coddling of the American Mind*, Allen Lane.

Acknowledgments

I would like to thank many of the people who have supported me to make this book possible:

To my mother, Donna, for her inspiration and unconditional love, and my father, Brooks, for challenging and supporting me to always grow to be my very best. To my brother, Mark, for being my buddy in the early years and for always striving to accept and love me for who I am. For my husband, Jeff, who has seen the value, beauty and potential in me since day one and who has been the most consistent support in my life. For my daughter, Madison, who helps me see through fresh eyes each and every day. I love and thank you all with the whole of my being.

Big thanks to all of the people who showed their belief in me by pre-ordering this book.

I also want to give heartfelt thanks to Lee Constantine for convincing me to write *Looking In* and for all he did to help it along. Finally, I want to express my deep gratitude to my friend, editor and publisher, Jennifer Bright, for being the most loving, helpful and supportive book doula a person could ever desire.

Photo credit: Randi Markowitz

About the Author

Traci Philips is an Executive Leadership and Performance Coach to visionary entrepreneurs and corporate executives. She uses her innate gift of decoding language to discover one's purpose and blocks to help clients develop more effective thinking, communication, resolution strategies, decision-making and leading during times of change and when the stakes are high. She is passionate about showing leaders how to create a more cohesive, cooperative experience and environment within their workplace cultures. Her ultimate goal is to support her clients to live authentically and lead powerfully by creating more awareness about who they are, how they want to impact others and what legacy they want to leave behind.

9 781952 481338